F?@K KNOWS

Shailendra Singh has B.T.D.T.—Been there. Done that. Some know him as a 'sports marketing guru', some as an 'advertising whizz' or 'Bollywood producer', and many acknowledge him as a shrewd 'dealmaker'. He's conceptualized the most famous and long-lasting campaigns for India's biggest brands, managed and helped adjust the jockstraps of India's most respected cricketers, and launched the careers and egos of the country's biggest celebrities. He's opened a direct line of communication with India's youth by creating massive music festivals, is emerging as Asia's largest music promoter, and has produced over sixty Bollywood movies. He has worked on awareness campaigns for HIV/AIDS, cancer and piracy. He enjoys short trots on the beach, any sport that uses a ball, and sugar. This is his first, and hopefully not last, attempt at writing a book.

F?@K
KNOWS

Shailendra Singh

RUPA

Published by
Rupa Publications India Pvt. Ltd 2013
7/16, Ansari Road, Daryaganj
New Delhi 110002

Sales centres:
Allahabad Bengaluru Chennai
Hyderabad Jaipur Kathmandu
Kolkata Mumbai

ISBN: 978-81-291-2388-6

10 9 8 7 6 5 4 3 2 1

The moral right of the author has been asserted.

Typeset in Dante 11/14.5

Printed and bound in India by Replika Press Pvt. Ltd.

To the Universe

CONTENTS

DISCLAIMER

Any resemblance to persons living or dead is totally intentional. For those dead, I'm sure it won't be a problem, for obvious reasons. For those living, please don't mind that I have used your real name and, in one case, your phone number (People won't really believe I did all this shit! Back me up, Asif!).

Everything that I have written about is totally true and absolutely happened. Except for the story about my uncle in Shamli. And, of course, the story about Ganesha. I made those up. And I may have based the story about Ayjaz on an old folk tale I heard somewhere. But, other than that, everything is true and accurate. I swear on my uncle in Shamli.

HOW TO READ THIS BOOK

1. Read only one chapter at a time. Take long breaks between chapters. The logic contained in this book is very intense and might disrupt your preconditioned assumptions about the world.
2. If you absolutely must read two chapters back to back, a neat vodka lime, a glass of Moët Rose, or a Kir Royale could help ease the brain pain.
3. If, for reasons only known to you, you have read three chapters of this book at the same time, you're totally screwed. I can't help you. No one can.
4. The best places to read this book, are:

    a. On the pot.
    b. On the iPad/eReader that you carry around in your man purse, at 2 a.m. in a nightclub while you wait for your buddies to climb off those two dancers.
    c. In bed, while pretending to be busy, so you don't have to make love to your fiancée of five years. (Hint: If it's taken so long to seal the deal, and you are avoiding sex with her, she is really not the one.)
    d. On a road trip, if you don't get carsick. Feel free to read chapters aloud to travel companions.
    e. On your BlackBerry Bold, under the boardroom table, while your boss is talking about the future direction of the

company. You could care less; you have already reached your targets for the year.

f. But the best place is on the pot.

5. Do not read this book on a flight. When the common sense of it gets too profound, you will have nowhere to run and hide. Besides, there is very bad language that will embarrass your neighbour as he reads over your shoulder.

PREFACE

This book is an accumulation of my life's lessons: my journeys, my anecdotes, my profound observations, my simple wisdom. I do not claim any objective understanding of the universal truth, with which I hope to save your soul. No, I'm just sharing what I have gathered up, or tripped over, along the way, in the hope that maybe you won't have to make the same mistakes. Or miss out on some really cool shit. If our collective learning can be compounded for the betterment of all mankind, well then, that's a bonus! So be it.

You kids are too smart these days, I agree. But my generation has been around the block a few times, and can point out a few things in the neighbourhood: the bench not to sit on because the nanny changes the baby's diaper there, the hot beta whose marriage is already secretly arranged, so you shouldn't bother chasing him, and the beti who pays her security guard not to tell her parents that she sneaks out at night. It's all useful info. Take it or leave it.

But, listen...if you happen to follow your heart, like I advise in this book, and it leads you into financial and emotional ruin, then you can't blame me. If you listen to your gut, as I suggest, and it tells you to quit that cushy job you have, take out a massive loan and open your own scuba diving shop in Chandigarh, well then, that's just plain stupid. You can't blame me for that. You may have misunderstood the message from your heart. Or, your execution was shit. You're new at this. You can't just expect to get it right the first time around.

So, got that? I don't claim to be a master or a life coach. I don't claim to have the answers. Actually, this whole book is about the fact that only you know the answers to your questions. Me? I'm just a cool dude, telling you cool things. I'm completely indemnified.

f?@k knows   **(FUK noze)** *phrase*

The true usage of the phrase is to claim that you simply 'do not know'. However, the phrase is often interpreted as 'F?@k Nose', which may cause offence to the listener. This misinterpretation is often replied to using 'Cunt Face' which is regarded as the appropriate answer.

'What time is Adam supposed be here?'
'F?@k knows.'
'Only asking...Cunt Face.'

[Urban Dictionary]

F?@K KNOWS

When I suffered a near heart attack on 24 November 2010, at the age of forty-five, I was happy to go. I was ready to call it quits. Cash in my chips. Kick the bucket. Bite the big one.

For quite a few years before my chest started to ache, I hadn't been enjoying my life. My idol, mentor and reason for living—my father—had died from cancer, and I had lost all direction. My body, which had been strong and dependable all my life, had started to fall apart in strange, stupid ways. My patience and energy had been exhausted in an epic battle for justice in a far-off Middle Eastern country. I had lost substantial amounts of hard-earned money in the 2008 economic crisis.

I was f?@king bored.

But, if I am honest with myself, which I am trying to be these days, then it started long before that. I hadn't been truly living, hadn't been the captain of my destiny, since the time I was a child. Since the time I began to understand human language. Since the time my father started to say 'you have to' and 'you must'.

'You have to go to school every day. You have to go to college. You must get good marks. You must get a respectable job. You have to get married as soon as you have settled into a career.' For each step up the staircase of my life, there was already an expectation. I didn't understand these expectations, but he was my father, and I loved him unconditionally. I did whatever he told me to do. And I did it well.

I wanted to become an athlete. He told me that was not respectable, and that I should become a businessman. I was only a second-class commerce graduate, and he used to tell me, 'You will never get a salary of over Rs 1,000 per month if you don't go into business and prove yourself.' He was right. My first job at the Shamiana coffee shop paid Rs 1,280. It wasn't even enough to get me three meals a day.

'Be a businessman. Join your older brother,' he said. My brother, Harry, had started an advertising firm. It was the first business venture of the Singh family. I joined, we were successful, and one day, we held a cheque of Rs 10 lakh in our hands. We had never seen Rs 10 lakh before. My father said, 'This is fantastic! Congratulations, boys! But you should get a crore.' We said, 'Yeah, okay.' And we earned a crore. My father said, 'Congratulations, boys! Fantastic work! But, you know, you should get 10 crores.' And we earned 10 crores. And then 100 crores. And 500 crores. It didn't stop.

We had 500 crores in the bank, but my father was setting aside a few lakhs every month. He wouldn't spend it. He wouldn't spend any of the money. 'What will happen if Percept shuts down? What will happen if you guys go broke?' my father would ask. I tried to explain to him that if we were going to go wrong with $100 million, his $1 million was not going to help us. But he felt that if we lost everything, he would at least be able to buy us some rice and daal. He said that it was his duty to always provide, but I saw through this to his insecurity and his fear. The fear of our failure was always hovering close by.

When I was wheeled into the intensive care unit that November night, I cared more about the fact that I hated hospitals than I cared about the fact that I might die. I had lost my father the year before and, like I said, I was kind of ready to go walk amongst the clouds and talk to him once again. 'I died young, but, dad, I accomplished everything that you dreamt for me in this life. I made lots of money, I married a lovely woman and had a beautiful son. I won national awards. I created brand new industries in the country. I set benchmarks. Aren't you proud of me, dad?'

He did it all out of love. He wanted the best for me. But the truth of the matter was that until that point, when I was stretched out on a stretcher in the hospital, I had lived my life for my father.

As the anaesthetic kicked in, I envisioned the conversation that I would have with my father when we walked together:

'Dad, did you know when I was born that I wouldn't be really smart?'

'F?@k knows, my son, but you made it through okay.'

'Dad, did you really think that I couldn't make it as a cricketer? I was so good!'

'F?@k knows, my son, but it wasn't a safe option.'

'Dad, did you know that I would be a good businessman when you told me to be one?'

'F?@k knows, my son, but that's what everyone else was doing.'

'Did you think that I would win a national award and make you proud?'

'F?@k knows, my son, but I'm happy that you did.'

I didn't write this book to preach and teach. I am not anyone to say that I know more about this life than you do. I really just thought that, maybe, if ten people read this book and are moved by it in some way, if they feel a connection with my journey, or with my mindset, and I can show them a different perspective, then I will be happy. Especially if that person is one of India's 600 million under the age of twenty-five. For you guys, a marginal shift in thinking, a slight change in attitude, can multiply over the years to increase your general level of happiness for a lifetime.

I don't give a flying monkey if this book ever becomes a bestseller. I do not aspire to be an intellectual. I want to be known as a creative moron who convinced a few people to break out of the bad habit of living their lives based on other people's expectations.

I want to inspire just a few people to follow their hearts. To live on their own terms. That's all. I regret the fact that, in my younger days, I did not follow my heart. At every juncture in my life, my heart had told me what to do, and I told it to be quiet. I listened to everyone but my own heart, and my heart slowly, slowly gave up, until the night that it finally, almost, gave in.

Still under anaesthetic, walking through the misty morning with my father, he turns to me and starts asking questions:

'Son, do you think things would have been better if you were smarter in school?'

'F?@k knows, dad. I seem to have ended up okay.'

'Son, do you really think that you would have made it as a professional cricket player?'

'F?@k knows, dad. But I sure should have tried.'

'Son, do you know why you are in this hospital room?'

'F?@k knows, dad! I was at a boot camp the day before this and feeling totally fine and fit!'

'Son…'

'Dad, f?@k knows anything about what might have been, or could have been or should have been. I realized just this moment that there are only two things that I really know the answer to: "Who am I?" and "What do I want?"'

I remembered those two questions when I came around in

the hospital room. I had plenty of time to think about them while on bed rest, and I realized that they were truer than anything that I had ever put my faith in.

The only real answer that I could give to any question, except for those two questions, was 'f?@k knows'. But those two questions—Who am I? What do I want?—f?@k! I knew the answers to those two! From the depths of my soul to the farthest reaches of the universe, I knew.

From that day forward, my life became very simple and very sexy. I started to follow my heart. And I started, finally, to live.

INTRODUCING ME,
TO MYSELF

I started reading books quite late in life. I was always way too busy. Especially for fiction. Each and every day, I live my own amazing tale, full of crazy characters and bizarre plot twists. I've never been interested in someone else's made-up story.

When I do find the time to pick up a book, usually between 5.30 and 7.30 a.m., when it's too early to start troubling people with my ideas and thoughts and business plans, I read non-fiction. I like biographies; the success stories of the world's powerful people, leaders and mentors. Great achievements are usually achieved after overcoming trauma or tremendous odds, which I find incredibly motivating.

I love quotes by famous people, successful people. Short, sweet, to the point. Bang in a big thought, in as few words as possible. Conciseness is an admirable art.

I also love the newageself-helpmotivationalcontemporary-spritualenlightenment books filling the bestseller lists these days. Deepak Chopra. Eckhart Tolle. Neale Donald Walsch. Most of what they write is highly theoretical and impractical, especially if you read it chapter by chapter. (You do realize what these authors are doing, right? They simply take a quote by a famous person—who, after a lifetime of learning was able to sum up their understanding in a short, but powerfully decisive statement—and expand upon it. They happily reprint the quote, and then...make it long again.)

I do find, though, that if I use the books like a lesson-of-the-day roulette wheel, I come up with great stuff. You know, close my eyes, pick a book from the shelf, flip to a page, open my eyes and read the first chapter I see.

Usually, the chapter is completely relevant to at least one out of the one hundred issues that I am dealing with at that moment. It's almost as if Robin Sharma is speaking directly to me. Like he knows me, understands my problem, and has the perfect solution for me.

It's a great way to refocus my mind on whatever it is I'm dealing with—a few words to encourage me to switch on the light of awareness inside, and expose the confusion. Usually, the answers to our problems are simple, but we choose not to see them, for some reason or the other. We need a little support, someone to hold our hand, and give us the strength to acknowledge the truth. Since true friends, understanding families and the time they have to spend with us these days are few and far between, Deepakji conveniently fills in.

I do learn a lot this way, I must admit. Refocus. Shine the light of awareness. Lately, what I've been consciously working on, and what I am coming to realize may be the most important accomplishment of my life is this: to *know* myself.

When I was younger, that was simply a given. What else was there to possibly know than what I currently knew? I knew who I was. I knew it all. I was Shailendra Singh.

But Eckhart Tolle kept telling me that I didn't know myself, that I was 'delusional' and would have to do my damnedest to get to know myself. That made me very nervous. It sounded very grown-up and mature. Like it was time to stop living and start reflecting. Go sit in a corner in the lotus position and meditate. Stop talking. Be silent. Find yourself.

F?@k off! Whenever I shut my eyes and shut my mouth, my mind would go mad thinking about women and sex and the newly released movie at the cinema. Hey, if that was the real me, then I was fine with that! No issues. No changes required.

But as I got older, issues did start to come to the surface. Nagging little questions. I had accomplished so much, made a shitload of money, had rich and powerful friends, threw massive parties and drove expensive cars. This was what I had wanted, right? Right?

But was this what I really wanted? Doubt started to creep in. I began to feel that I was missing something. Hadn't I wanted to be an athlete, not a businessman? Didn't I used to envision myself as a creative genius, and not the dealmaker that I was best known as?

Deepak and Robin and Oprah told me that I had doubts because I didn't really know myself. They advised me to find myself. Since I wasn't going to sit in a corner meditating, I decided that a good start to knowing myself would be to literally see myself.

I went to the mirror. I looked deep into my own eyes, and said hello to myself. 'Hello, Shailendra. Tell me about yourself.' And when I did that, I realized that for all these years I hadn't ever really known myself. I hadn't been honest with myself. I had never really understood my true nature and what I wanted from myself. What I wanted from my life. Searching the depths of my soul, I realized that...

Oh, balls, I'm not fooling you at all, am I? I never did that. Who does that? Who really wakes up every morning and looks at themselves in the mirror for so long? Are you that in love with yourself?

Okay, but wait. Shit. I promised that I would do my best not to lie in this book. Seriously? I have done it. I don't care, call me a narcissist. But I have done it, a few times. I still do it. And it's f?@king brilliant.

After I get past noticing the nostril hair I have to trim, the ear hair I should also trim, the slowly receding hairline, and the fact that I should probably go to the dentist, I start to focus. At first, staring deep into my own eyes, I see an alien peering back. It frickin' freaks me out. 'That's not me! Who the hell is that?' Scary shit.

But then I get used to myself. I start to converse with myself. I forget about all the books, the online research, the influence of my family and friends, and I ask myself for answers. I ask myself if I am happy, and the answer comes shockingly fast. The answers to 'why not?' come a little more slowly, but they do come.

Don't be shy, f?@ker. I admitted that I do it. So there's no reason why you shouldn't do it, too. Have a chat with yourself in the bathroom mirror. Ask yourself all the questions that nag you when you are falling asleep at night. Trust me, you'll get the most truthful answers from yourself.

Everything that you always wanted to know, everything that you didn't even know you wanted to know, everything that you need to know, is all right there inside of you. It's that easy.

I wish I had figured this shit out earlier.

F?@K KNOWS HOW *YOU AND I* BECAME *F?@K KNOWS*

'I WAS ALIVE YESTERDAY.
DEAD TODAY.
F?@K KNOWS ABOUT TOMORROW.'

The journey of writing this book actually began five years ago. I felt as though I had already lived a few lifetimes in my four decades, and I wanted to share my thoughts on the matter. Everyone I know told me that I was too young to write a book. But when I took stock of all my experiences, moments I had been witness to, lessons I had learnt, I was sure that I had something to say. Why did I have to wait until I was old and crippled and about to die, to write a book? I had something to say, and I wanted to say it right then.

I wasn't really sure *how* I was going to write it; my lessons weren't learnt from books. The truth is, the reason that I have never read a single book cover to cover, in all my life, is because I'm dyslexic. Dyslexia makes it really difficult to read page to page, chapter to chapter. I just don't have the patience.

Even without any deep knowledge of books or literature, I decided I was just going to jump right in and see what happened. Just get my thoughts down on paper and worry about the rest later. Here's a second confession for you. In forty years, I have never used a computer. Never opened a laptop, never sent an email, never used a BlackBerry. I figured I would write the book the good old-fashioned way, with pencil and paper. My dyslexia makes my chicken scratch totally illegible but I started scribbling anyway, hoping my thoughts could one day be translated into something structured and legitimate.

The title of that first book was *You and I.*

Throughout my life, dyslexia, combined with my lack of technological skills, resulted in quite a brilliant phenomenon. Finding it too difficult to study books, I was forced, in school and afterwards, to learn through observation, personal experience, and interactions with others. Without letters and emails, I had to communicate personally, one on one, and then develop those interactions into relationships.

Relationships have always been my driving force. They are how I function. I have built thousands of relationships with clients, suppliers, talent, media, friends…everyone. From business tycoons and millionaires, to celebrities and athletes, to cab drivers and office boys, it has been my personal relationship with each one of them that has allowed me to succeed in whatever I set out to do.

You and I was going to be a collection of essays on the topic of relationships, written by some of the people closest to me. People with whom I had travelled a part of my journey. I wanted to gather and share their thoughts and wisdom on what it meant to have a relationship in this digital networking day and age.

I registered the name with the Indian trademark office and designed the cover of the book. You know how some people, especially in Asian cultures, keep a single goldfish in a bowl on their desk for good luck? I, personally, cannot fathom how it can be 'good luck' to keep a living creature in complete isolation in a tiny glass bowl all its life, swimming in endless circles, watching the outside world travel past it, with no hope of ever getting anywhere.

My book cover showed one such lonely goldfish, risking his life to jump from his bowl into the bowl of his lonely neighbour on the next desk. 'F?@k this shit, I don't want to be alone any more!' the thought bubble read.

No one wants to be alone. In success or failure, illness or happiness, grief or celebration, no one wants to be alone. We are social creatures, and we need communication, understanding and love to survive. In order to thrive. *You and I* was about the relationships that had allowed me to thrive.

The first person whom I requested to write a chapter was the person with whom I had the most highly valued relationship in my life—my father. His chapter, however, ended up reading more like a letter of recommendation from a very satisfied father than an essay on relationships. It wasn't entirely what I was looking for, but it was incredibly touching. It proved once again that my father was my biggest fan.

I wrote to all my friends, across the planet, requesting them to send me their thoughts on relationships. Responses started to flow in. The book was shaping up nicely.

And, then… Bam! A series of events unfolded that changed the course of my book, and my life. Things I couldn't have ever imagined happening, happened.

My father, who stood 6'2" tall, a strong man with village roots, the rock of my existence, was diagnosed with fourth stage lung cancer. Just like that. One day, happy and teasing the eldest of his five grandkids that it was time to find a nice girl and get married. The next day, visiting the doctor because of a loss of appetite, and being told that he had three months to live.

My idol, my mentor, my entire life, held my hand and cried, 'My son, I don't want to die. Do something. Save me.'

During those months of heartbreaking agony, watching my

father die slowly, two important people in my life had a serious misunderstanding with a very confused Arab nation. It was a two-year-long battle in defence of the truth. In a triumph of epic proportions, we eventually emerged victorious, their innocence was proved beyond all reasonable doubt, but the misunderstanding took its toll on me. Shocked that something like this could even happen and shattered with the effort of such an intense fight, I was beyond exhausted—in body, mind and soul.

In my entire life, I hadn't suffered a single illness or injury. I have always been an avid athlete and a very health-conscious guy. But, a few days after returning from the Middle East, I collapsed at the airport. My left leg had become totally incapacitated due to my spinal discs pressing against my sciatic nerve. My doctor ordered 24/7 bed rest for two months, a depressing sentence for a man of my stamina and energy. After recovering, it happened again. Another two months in bed.

I busted my eardrums during a faulty sound test at a music festival. My left thumb was totally shattered in a tough cricket match. I, who had once chosen to be forever disfigured rather than go to the hospital to have a broken arm reset, had to have a six-hour-long operation to save the thumb. And, to top it all off, I also managed a near fatal heart attack with 95 per cent blockage in the main artery.

I managed to save my close friends from a decade of imprisonment, my thumb from falling off, and my heartbeat from fully stopping, but I couldn't save my father. He passed away eleven months after he had been diagnosed with cancer.

Why did I have to lose my father? Why did I have to fight so hard for the freedom of my best friends? Why did I have to fall to pieces from the effort? Why didn't my heart stop beating the day I fell sick? What was I supposed to do now?

Through all my darkest moments, through my recovery, and through all my asking, I only found one answer to all of my questions: 'F?@k knows.'

F?@K IT LIST

'IT'S JUST LIKE A BUCKET LIST,
BUT WITH A COOLER NAME.'

Call me corny—I don't give a flying monkey—I was really inspired after watching the *The Bucket List*, starring Morgan Freeman and Jack Nicholson as two dying, miserable assholes. It's become quite a household term—'bucket list'. You hear it all the time. There are websites dedicated to the idea of sharing your bucket-list items. There are books written about what should be on your list. A lot of people mock the concept and make a joke of it, but you can only make fun of something that is popular, otherwise the joke isn't funny.

I think the bucket list is a goddamn brilliant exercise.

You're too young to have a bucket list, you say? F?@k off. You'll soon realize that life without a destination can be quite unruly and unrewarding. You can wait until the day you look back and regret that you didn't accomplish some simple things that you wanted to in this shorter-than-you-think life, or you can put your ego aside for a bit right now, and listen.

Would it help if we called it something else? Would 'F?@k It List' sound better? As in, 'F?@k it! These are the things that I am going to do in this life, and nothing will stand in my way.' Better? F?@k It List it is, then.

After you introduce yourself to yourself—by conversing with

yourself in the mirror every morning (I know you all went and actually did it, and realized how enlightening it is), finding out what you like and don't like, who you are and what you want to be—the next logical step is to find out what it is you want out of this life.

Don't be too cool. Don't start off saying that you want to oust all the bloodthirsty dictators in the world, end terrorism or bring about world peace. If you are reading this book, you probably aren't the type to see those ones through. Start with the simple things.

Although I hope you will find it difficult to put this book down, you should do so and go sit at your desk and write out the five things that you want accomplish by the end of the year. Not what your family wants you to do, or your wife wants you to do, or your boss wants you to do. What you, deep down in your heart, really want to do. Seriously...do it. Make your F?@k It List right now.

Done? Feel good? But now, my friend, please realize that, unlike most of the self-help books that you might have read, what I am suggesting you do is not an abstract exercise. I actually expect you to go and do it. Simple as that. 'Just do it', as the Nike logo commands you to do—those copywriters for Nike were f?@king brilliant!

Just do it. I know it's easier said than done. We are so used to putting aside our desires and goals in order to handle the immediate issues that come and go in our daily lives. Just like our New Year's resolutions. Before you know it, the year is up, and you realize that you never did sign up at the gym, you still take two sugars in your coffee and have put on eight kilos!

You can't let that happen to your F?@k It List. You have to put in a little effort to not get sidetracked from your goals. You have to wake up every morning and say, 'F?@k it! No matter what, I am going to move one step closer to fulfilling my goals!'

You'll be surprised at just how simple your desires are. How easy it is to make something happen when you are completely sure that it is what you want. And how just a few ordinary things can give you extraordinary happiness, if they happen to be the things that you want.

Watch the movie again. Make your F?@k It List. Go out and get it done. This life is about you. It's time to live it on your terms.

If you are not living to make the most of being alive, what are you living for?

MATH OF ME TIME

'WORK HARD. PARTY HARDER.
LIVE HARDEST.'

Okay, let's do some simple math. Let's take the twenty-four hours in a day… Well, actually, that's quite misleading, isn't it? There are only twelve hours in a day. And twelve hours in a night.

So, let's consider twenty-four hours in a day/night cycle. In that day/night cycle, how many hours do you invest in yourself? How much of that time is really *your* time?

Most people sleep about seven hours, which is important for health reasons. $24 - 7 = 17$ hours. Subtract the nine hours you are at work. I used to work a lot more than nine hours. And actually work. I don't touch the computer, so I'm not playing solitaire or checking Facebook. I don't smoke, so no smoke breaks. I'm the joint managing director, so I can't sit with colleagues and bitch about the bosses. I've only just recently realized the gastrological benefits of taking a proper, quiet break to eat and digest lunch. But let's go with the average—nine hours of work a day.

(If you work more than nine hours a day, more than being super ambitious, it probably just means that you are not focusing and working efficiently in those hours to complete your work. Telling your friends that you work fourteen hours a day is not a badge of pride. They probably just think you are really stupid.

If you work more than nine hours a day, you better be well on your way to curing cancer or ending world hunger. Otherwise, it's just not healthy.)

So 17 – 9 = 8 hours. Let's subtract sixty minutes of travel time. Ninety minutes, if you have to catch a rickshaw, find a cab and commute on the full f?@king havoc of the Mumbai roadways, or take a train or bus.

Subtract fifteen minutes for a shower and nose-hair trim. Ten minutes to get dressed. Twenty minutes of loo breaks throughout the day. (Thirty minutes if you are playing 'Angry Birds' on the pot and leaving with a giant ring around your ass.) Ten minutes deciding what you are going to order for dinner and from where, twenty minutes watching *Big Boss* before it's delivered and ten minutes to wolf it down and leave the dishes in the sink to wash up later or for the maid if you have one. Shall we say sixty minutes a day for necessary errands like grocery shopping, paying your household bills, reassessing your health insurance, checking your messages on shaadi.com or waiting in line at the BlackBerry store to fix the broken tracker ball on your phone?

Subtract thirty-five minutes for gossip time: the morning phone call from your mother asking you how much money you lost the day before, the afternoon phone call from your best buddy requesting you to please tell his wife that he was with you the night before last, the phone call from your favourite restaurant's maître d' to tell you that four of your employees are ordering champagne and cranberry vodkas for a table full of questionable women. 'I regret to inform you that they signed your name on the bill, sir.'

Go ahead, show me your processing power—how much time are you left with?

If, like me, you have a lovely wife and a domestic help to do all the cooking and cleaning, then you are left with three-and-a-half hours. 210 minutes. 12,600 seconds.

That's the time you have to focus on yourself, on a typical weekday. How do you use those 210 minutes? A good run on the treadmill and weightlifting at the gym? A Bollywood movie? A few hours on the couch, with your hand down your pants, watching some mindless television sitcoms? Buy One Get One Free beers at TGIF in the mall? Surfing the internet, reading celebrity gossip? Curled up and reading a good book, like this one?

And that's being generous. If you have a girlfriend, a boyfriend, a husband, a wife, children, in-laws, then you have, like, what? Maybe seven minutes in a day completely to yourself?

How much do you really value this time?

You know the old saying: nobody on his or her deathbed ever looks back and wishes they had worked more. It's never, 'I wish that I had spent more hours in the office, crunching numbers, filing papers and sending emails.' It's certainly not, 'I wish that I had watched more reality TV, seen every episode of CSI, or watched every Jennifer Lopez movie.'

You're young. You think you're damn cool, which I agree that you probably are if you are reading this book. You think that you have all the time in the world, but, if you do the math, you realize you only have a few precious minutes in every day to make the most of it.

You better bang it in, boys and girls.

MATH OF LIFE

F?@k knows why we live as though we are going to live forever. We're not going to. We're going to die. We all know this, but we don't really believe it. It's only when we really believe that we will die, that we start living fully.

The average life expectancy of a person born in India is 64.7 years. If you live in Mumbai, it's 56.8 years of age. (The retirement age for government pensioners in the country is sixty years. Go figure.)

We calculated the basic Math of Me Time in the previous chapter, which was supposed to encourage you to value the time available to you on any given day. That didn't seem to have much of an impact on you, did it? What have you changed in your life since reading that chapter? Nothing? Yeah, I thought so. Ass.

So, let's look at it another way. Bang in the point a little more. Make you believe. Let's do a simple calculation regarding the amount of time that you have in your life to be awake and focused on *you*—the things you want to do, experience and accomplish.

I'm going to start the calculation with the life expectancy of the average Mumbaikar, because, hell, it's the fourth most populous city in the world and they're/I'm already eight years behind India's average. (F?@k. Eight years of my life, lost, because I choose to live in the commercial and entertainment capital—

'India's richest city'. I will consider the definition of 'rich' in a later chapter.)

Okay, so, let's start with 56.8 years to live.

Let's not count the first five years of your life, because you're not really that conscious of what the hell is going on, and can't even wipe your own ass. If we round that figure up to 5.8, it will make our math easier: 56.8 years − 5.8 unconscious years = 51 conscious, productive years to live.

The general consensus is that most people get between six to eight hours of sleep a night. Let's take an average of seven hours of sleep a night, out of twenty-four hours, which is 29.2 per cent of your day. Of your fifty-one years, 29.2 per cent is about fifteen years. Subtract fifteen from fifty-one, and you're left with thirty-six years awake.

For sixteen years, from the age of five to twenty-one, you *have* to go to school and college. An Indian child averages 224 days at school (upper primary). That's 16 years x 224 days a year = 3,584 days. An article in *The Times of India* says that, on average, kids spend eight to ten hours in school each of those days. Let's go with nine hours as an average. So:

9 hours a day x 224 school days in a year
= 2,016 hours in a year
2,016 hours in a year x 16 years = 32, 256 hours of your life
32,256 hours / 8,760 hours in a year
= 3.68 years of your life at school.
36 years awake − 3.68 years at school
= 32.32 years awake and not staring at a chalkboard.

As soon as you toss your cap in the air, you have to get a job to start paying back your loans or supporting your parents, who now want to retire. Conservatively, let's say one spends nine hours a day working, five days a week. (I know all you Mumbaikars are cracking up—you work more than nine hours and on weekends—but, in taking an average, we have to consider our government workers' forty-hour work weeks, as well.) With say, twenty-seven vacation and sick days, you have 234 days to go to work, that is thirty-three weeks. So:

9 hours a day x 5 working days = 45 hours per week
45 hours x 33 weeks = 1,485 hours in a year
1,485 x (51 years – 21 years spent studying)
                 = 44,550 hours of your life
44,550 hours/8,760 hours in a year = 5.08 years

Subtract the final 5.08 years from your 32.32 years and you are left with 27.24 years awake, and not slogging for a paycheck.

Let's calculate the daily routine: thirty minutes a day in the bathroom (more if you have a stack of *Calvin and Hobbes* beside the pot or you have to walk down to the train tracks for some privacy); an hour and a half for eating meals (assuming you have a cook to prepare it, and you're only eating it); shall we say one hour getting suited, shined and styled for work, and then taking it all off again after the long day? That is:

3 hours a day eating and prepping x 365 days in a year
        = 1,095 hours a year
1,095 hours a year x 51 years = 55,845 hours in your life
55,845 hours in your life/8,760 hours in a year = 6.4 years
27.24 years awake and not working – 6.4 years eating, shitting and styling = 20.84 years left.

If you spend less than forty-five minutes commuting one way to work in Mumbai, then you are exceptionally blessed.

351 hours (1.5 hours a day commuting x 234 working days)
x 30 working years = 10,530 hours
10,530 hours/8,760 hours in a year = 1.2 years commuting.
20.84 years − 1.2 years = 19.64 taxi-less, train-less years to
thrive.

You're left with 19.64 years of living on your own time, on
your own terms, and this doesn't include waiting in queues or
the time spent on trying to solve daily problems. 19.64 years to
fulfil all of your dreams and desires for this lifetime. 19.64 years
to surrender to the whims and fancies of your existence. 19.64
years to be who you want to be.

Oh shit! Sorry. Wait. Don't forget... If you are twenty-five
years old right now, then you have already lived half of your
overall life, and half of your 'me-time life'.

Can you hear that clock ticking a little more loudly now?
That's the beauty of clocks: as it keeps track of advancing time,
it also counts down the time that you have left. You've got 9.82
years left.

It's not as much time as you thought, huh? And, we haven't
even factored in the time given over to your husband, wife,
children or golden retriever! We haven't calculated for times of
sickness. Or time spent at the dentist or gynaecologist's office. Or
the time spent trying to understand your bank statement, credit
card bill, loan repayment schedule, mobile phone bill, cable and
internet bundling options, and frequent flier mile usage rules
and regulations.

It's a little scary when you break it down, isn't it? These
calculations are just my approximations. You should do your own
math. Add it up. Subtract it down. If I had known at the start,
that I really only had nineteen years of time in my life, I would

have done things a lot differently.

My advice? Don't wait until you are sixty years old to make your F?@k It List. At sixty, you'll feel damn proud that you beat the 56.8 average, but you'll be too tired and decrepit to do most of the things on your list. (Also, all the rainforests will have been razed for McDonald's farmland, the glaciers on Kilimanjaro will have all melted, and there'll be no other languages to learn because everyone will speak English by then.)

I highly recommend that you make a yearly F?@k It List. Or better yet, a monthly F?@k It List. Hell, make a daily F?@k It List. And start now. Plan selfishly. Plan every moment of your life in a manner that gives you maximum happiness and maximum satisfaction. Monitor the profit and loss account of your life as diligently as you balance the profit and loss account of your company.

Only then, when your clock finally stops ticking, can you say goodbye to this life knowing that you have made the most of it. Content that you have lived your life to the fullest, in the way that you chose to live it.

Only then can you dive into that grave, with a few backflips and a huge, shit-eating grin on your face. Don't roll in, limp, mumbling protests and grumpy with regrets.

Get life, before it gets you.

BORN WITH A HEART

'WARNING: YOUR BRAIN IS CONSTANTLY MAKING UNCONSCIOUS
DECISIONS ON YOUR BEHALF.'

When a newborn pops out of a mother's vajayjay, everyone celebrates. A child is born! Family crowds around to see, friends bring flowers, sweets are eaten. A new life has arrived!

But the mother has been celebrating this new life within her for quite some time. Since the moment that she first felt the child's heartbeat within her. When she first heard the fetal heartbeat on the monitors at the gynaecologist's. That heartbeat was a sign of life. Her baby, still unborn, was nevertheless alive.

When the heart stops beating, you stop being alive. Simple as that. No heartbeat? No chance. You're done. Deceased. Dead. Departed. Game over.

The heart is what wakes you up, and what puts you to sleep forever. F?@k knows why we don't *live* by our hearts.

Your heart is your alpha and your omega. More than anything, your heart has your best interests at…well…heart. It's the centre of your universe. Your heart is where your soul lives.

Can't you feel it?

Is there anything greater than feeling the first tugs of love on your heart? The unceasing joy in your heart upon finding your soulmate? Holding your newborn baby in your arms and realizing that your heart beats for that child for the rest of his or her life?

Or giving up a sure thing, to follow the gentle whisper of your heart, and finding yourself on top of the world?

If you haven't followed your heart, given it over to someone, had it shattered and thrown back at you, felt it fall in love again, heard it sing when your tiny rescued kitten cuddled up under your chin and fell asleep, well, then…what the hell have you been doing?

Can you even hear your heart?

Even if you can tune out the din of the traffic, or the elevator music in the elevator, or the TV shouting in the other room, or your BlackBerry beeping at you all the time, then what you are left with is an even more consuming background noise.

Your mind. It never stops. That ceaseless inner dialogue. You usually don't notice that it's even there, until everything else goes quiet. It's the background noise to your life.

Your own voice, rattling around inside your head, drowns out the sure, steady, but mild voice of your heart.

Your ego has pitched camp in your mind. It bullies the heart around. The slow, burning, deep desire that you feel at your very core comes from the heart. The mind's favorite pastime is to f?@k that up with a campaign of fear: 'Why should you have that? You don't deserve that! Shouldn't you want that thing? They're all going to laugh at you. You can't handle the truth!'

'What do I do about this?' you ask? 'How do I shut off the mind, and listen to the heart?'

Who the f?@k knows?!

I just know that you have to try. You have to find the way to do it. I know that if you follow your heart, you will be headed in the right direction. I know that your heart will not lie to you. And I know that if you listen to your heart, you will have no regrets. I've known this for a while, but I've just started to actually do it. And it feels f?@king awesome.

Your heart is the closest thing to the truth that you will find in life. Your heart tells it to you straight. If you listen to your heart, you will find what it is you are looking for. If you follow your heart, you will find the answer, before you even asked the question.

In April 2012, in Argentina, a woman by the name of Analia Bouter gave birth to a baby girl, three months premature. Doctors could not identify a heartbeat, declared the baby dead and sent it straight to the morgue. Twelve hours later and with the baby's death certificate in hand, Analia and the baby's father were adamant that they be able to see the child one last time, and take a photo. They absolutely refused to leave until they saw their baby. They needed to say goodbye.

The father had difficulty opening the cold coffin lid, but when they did, the tiny baby cried out. Analia fell to her knees. Her husband was in total shock. The hospital staff freaked out. Four months later, although the baby is still seriously ill, her condition is stable.

If the parents hadn't listened to the insistent urging in their hearts to see their child one last time, they never would have discovered the neglected heartbeat in their miracle baby.

YOUR GUT IS ALWAYS RIGHT

'LEARN TO TRUST YOURSELF.
YOU'LL SLEEP BETTER AT NIGHT.'

First you have to find your gut. Medically and technically, your gut is another name for the entire gastrointestinal tract which starts at your mouth and ends at your anus. Your food processor, complete with waste disposal system. If you saw the film *The Human Centipede*, you know exactly what I mean. (If you didn't see the movie, consider yourself incredibly lucky, and for Christ's sake, do not Google it.)

Figuratively, your gut is that place deep inside your stomach, just below your belly button and above your crotch. Make sure you keep your focus *above* the crotch; it's too easy to get distracted downward.

The gut has always been considered the source of intuition. Where instinct lives. It also seems to be the source of bravery, providing the strength to battle seemingly insurmountable odds. You know, 'to have the guts' to do something.

But in recent times, technological and medical advancements have 'proven' that the brain is actually the source of all thoughts, emotions and feelings. The significance and power of the gut was demoted to an idiom. 'My "gut feeling" is that this match is fixed.' 'I hate his guts.' 'It takes "some guts" for that chick to walk up in here in that short-ass dress and those f?@k-me pumps.'

You can't blame us for falling for the research, because, who was doing the research? The mind! The brain was questioning, hypothesizing, probing and proving. Of course it was going to say that it was the best!

The brain said, 'Screw the gut, it's just a waste management system. I'm the smart one! The thinker, the feeler, the source of everything. I'm the king of the world!' And we said, 'Ah, right-o then. I'll just ignore all these feelings in my gut. It's probably just gas.'

But recently, science has brought some new facts to light. Turns out the gut is actually much more than a digestive organ. It does affect our mental state. Scientists have started calling it the 'second brain'.

They've discovered that there are more neurons located in a nine-metre section of the gut than are found in the spinal cord or the brain. And, even more tellingly, 90 per cent of your body's serotonin—your happy juice—is made in your gut. There is a direct line, a nerve, from your gut to your brain, and surprisingly, messages most often travel from the gut to the brain. Some of your strongest emotions, some of your happiest feelings, may actually come from the same place your shit is made. How awesome is that?

Science may have flip-flopped in its understanding of the gut, but did you ever have a doubt?

Remember when you were really young, let's say five years old, and your mum gave you two rupees to go to the candy store and pick whatever you wanted? You would strut in there with your two rupees and pick your favourite in a flash. You knew what you wanted. It was your gut that was saying, 'That's the one I like!'

Or that time when you had a strange feeling, for no reason,

that you were going to get fired that day, and had just deleted your porn folder (named—'quarterly reports', because who would ever check there?), the emails you had sent to your competitor asking for a job, and the Photoshopped images of your boss bound and gagged in a scene from *Dexter*, when office security came to escort you out of the building.

Your gut is the voice of the heart. Through messages, compulsions and split-second impulses from the gut, the heart steers you in the direction of your deepest desires and wishes. The heart, more deeply connected and aware than any of us realize, understands the bigger picture of what's happening around you, your role in the larger game, and sends warning signals, cautions, or encouragement, through the gut.

If you follow your gut, you will have no regrets. You'll be following your purest intent. As with anything, start with the simple things. Try it out and see for yourself. It works. As you pull out the chair at the next restaurant you go to, in the half-second before your bum slaps down on the seat, ask your gut, what do you want to eat? The very first thing you think of in that split second is what you really want. Choice made. Decision reached.

After your bum hits the wood, and you realize it's still warm from the last person who sat there, you shouldn't think about your meal any more. If you think about it more, it won't be your gut talking. It won't be the desire of your heart. At that point, it's your mind stepping in, asking questions, raising doubts and telling you: 'But what about...?' 'Maybe the...?' 'If I order that, my date will think I'm...'

In one f?@king flash of a second, you've lost the opportunity of doing exactly what you want to do, what's right for you. And you'll feel the difference.

If you order your first impulsive choice, you will get amazing energy from that meal. You'll be satisfied. If you let your mind make the decision, a thousand questions and reasons flashing through your mind before you even order, your stomach will have already reached acute levels of acidity and your digestion will be all f?@ked up. You won't leave that restaurant satisfied.

You've got to pay more attention to that first impulse. That first reaction of what you want, what you feel is right. You have to catch that, and hold on to it and not let your mind talk you out of it. The trick is, at the point the mind starts to speak up, you have to pause. Don't act. The mind is going to ask you to act. Don't act. Pause.

Don't think in that pause. Let your mind go blank. Let your feelings take over, and then go with it. It's that control over that pause that is the big play. It's the pause that you have to master. Your mind will produce many thoughts but in the quietness of that pause you can go back to your gut feeling, back to the message of your heart.

And, just one more time, for good measure, it's the area *above* the crotch. Ignore the messages from your crotch.

SHUT THE F?@K UP

'TOO MUCH INFORMATION, TOO MUCH KNOWLEDGE,
TOO MUCH NOISE—TELL YOUR MIND TO
"SHUT THE F?@K UP!"'

If your heart speaks the desires of your soul, and your gut speaks the language of the heart, then your mind speaks utter rubbish. Not only does it spew crap, it also hijacks the pure language of your heart and gut, twists it, distorts it and frickin' shoves it back down your throat like it's the truth.

A zillion rubbish thoughts are flowing through your mind every second, every minute, of every day. Imagine if you spoke out loud every thought that was running through your head, as you were thinking it. Every thought that passed through your mind, unfiltered and exposed. You would be called a 'f?@king lunatic' and thrown out on to the streets to live in a cardboard box. You would be 'that guy' in the train, telling everyone that God doesn't give a f?@k about them and they should just listen to the message of the ocean and get ready for the coming of the flowers.

In actuality, you really are just like 'that guy'. You have just as many ridiculous thoughts, misguided assumptions, and unanswered questions. You just keep your mouth shut and don't let anyone know. You're just better than him at pretending to be normal.

The mind's inane banter never ceases. When you went out to lunch yesterday, were you 'living in the moment'—focused on the smells, the flavours, the tastes of the dishes you selected? No. You were thinking about what you were going to do post-lunch—head straight back to office or hit up the Armani sale? You were wondering why the woman in the cubicle across yours was bitching about you to the receptionist, why your girlfriend didn't call you back, and if you wore your shirts one size smaller, would you look more like that beefy guy sitting at the table next to you in the skintight Under Armour?

They say the key to enlightenment is detachment. Detaching oneself from desire and from the mind. Disassociating from mind-generated thoughts. Stop identifying with them, because they are not you. They are not your true essence. Your true essence has to become the watcher of those thoughts. To become a watcher, you have to take a step back and see them for what they really are.

Thoughts are parasites. They don't have a life of their own. They feed off of you. They make themselves a part of you. They stay close to you, make you identify with them, make you believe that they are a part of you, so that you don't notice them and try to get rid of them. If you got rid of them, they would die.

Like the Cymothoa exigua. Heard of this creature? It's a parasite crustacean that enters a fish (usually a snapper) through the gills and attaches itself to the base of the fish's tongue. It proceeds to suck all the blood out of the tongue, which then shrivels up, dies and falls off. (Note: It's only the female Cymothoa exigua that does this.) A tongue-less fish won't be able to eat, which wouldn't be good for the Cymothoa exigua, so the friggin' thing then goes and attaches itself to the muscles of the tongue stub. The fish can then use the parasite like its own tongue and keep eating.

Yeah. Gross, right?

That's what thoughts are like. They are so embedded in you, that you think it *is* you. You don't realize that they are alien invaders that you need to get rid of. Not that the fish could do anything about it once it realized what was happening (no hands to pluck it out). But that's the beauty of being a further evolved species. We can become the observers. We can step back, see the parasitic thoughts for what they are, shine the light of awareness on them, and dissolve them. Be rid of them.

Then—F?@K—you've arrived! Transcended. Enlightened.

And you won't have a bug for a tongue.

A TIP

This is not from 'the author' of this book. No publishing house would let a real 'author' print this. This is a tip from Shailendra Singh, the man:

Look around you, what is it that we have that animals don't have? All the animals that we eat—goats, cows, fishes, pigs, chickens, lobsters? They have two eyes, two ears (except for lobsters), kidneys, livers (even lobsters), pancreases and hearts. What they don't have is a voice.

It is an unwritten law in nature—if you can't protest, you're fair game.

You better speak up, before you are eaten up.

MIND AS TECHNOLOGY

'USE YOUR MIND, DON'T LET IT USE YOU.'

Okay, so you're convinced that you should stop all those psycho thoughts that are constantly streaming through your head all day? You want to put an end to the mental noise and learn the art of being silent, so that in the silence, you can finally hear your own heart?

Then stop believing the mind is you. Stop identifying with its endless rambling. Stop identifying with its ego. It's not you. It's not your essence. It's not your real nature.

Think of your mind as a technological gadget. A biotechnological gadget. An organic CPU that is able to handle high-level computations and feed you analysis, but only if you ask it to. (CPU—central processing unit? No idea? Hmmm...)

Okay, how about this: the mind is like a carbon-based smartphone. It's portable. It's wireless. It's modular. It runs different apps at the same time, while other apps work quietly in the background to maintain smooth operations. Sometimes the apps conflict with each other and the process freezes up. Sometimes you run out of RAM. Every so often you need to upgrade to the latest version.

If your mind is a gadget, then it's nothing but a tool, and you have to be in control of it. You have to shut down a few of the apps when there are too many running. You probably shouldn't be running the 'How to Tell a Girl You Like Her' app while you are running your 'Calculus Reference' app while sitting for your final exams. You should pause the 'Last Night's Binge Drinking Photo Album' app while you are using your 'The Art of Negotiation' app in the Monday morning meeting.

For ultimate control, man over machine, you have to be able to shut the whole system down. Slide to Power Off. Press and hold the End/Power Key. Switch to airplane mode to avoid any outside interference.

Forget about staring into a candle and staring at a dot on the wall. If you want to focus—for meditation, for silence—just walk yourself through the process of shutting down all your apps, one at a time. Shut down the timeline, listing everything that happened in your past. Shut down the 'Expectation' app—of what you are expecting in the future. (If possible, you should totally 'uninstall' that app.) Mute your inner dialogue. Set all notifications to silent.

I know it's not easy for you guys. You can barely do these things with your real, lifeless gadgets.

Face it, you are f?@king addicted to those phones and iPads and iPods. Always staring down into your laps under the table, bending your necks at an awkward angle, pretending to be polite. Getting anxious when there is no little red light flashing on your BlackBerry. 'No one loves me?' Sleeping with it resting on the other pillow, with your Facebook page open just so you don't miss something. You suffer agonizing withdrawal symptoms when you leave your phone at home. You feel nauseous when you log off Twitter.

Just like you are addicted to all your real-life gadgets, you are addicted to your mind. Addicted to thinking.

It's not going to be easy, but you have to assume control over your mind in the same way. Have some discipline. More than you have with your phone. Know when you should be polite, put it on silent and hide it in your purse. Start using the right apps. Turn the speaker volume down so you don't hurt your ears. Know when to turn it off so you can actually have an uninterrupted night's sleep.

Even if you don't use the Power-Off switch on your phone, you know where it is. If your phone freezes and you can't work the Power-Off switch, you even know that you can take out the battery and reboot the whole system.

Find the Power-Off switch for your mind. It's there. I promise you. Find it.

And, the sooner, the better—before the whole system freezes up and your battery needs to be removed. You don't get a reboot.

THEY

When my eighteen-year-old niece decided that she wanted to work in the real world for a while, before she went on to further studies, I told her she would have to come in for an interview, just like everyone else.

When she arrived and sat down across from me at my desk, I asked her the question that I ask every new applicant. 'What do you want to do with your life?'

'I want to be a fashion designer,' was her instant answer.

'Ah, well then, be that,' I said. 'Why do you want to work here?'

'They won't let me,' she said.

I gasped, my eyes widened and I grabbed her hand and dragged her out on to the terrace outside my office. 'Who are they?' I asked, panic-stricken. 'Where are they? Are they listening to us? Are they watching us right now? WHO ARE THEY?'

After she recovered a bit, she said, 'No, no, no, chachu (uncle). I meant my parents. My parents will never allow me to do what I want to do.'

So I said, 'Oh, that's terrible. Why wouldn't your parents let you do what you want to do?'

Back in the office, we had a long conversation about that over a cup of coffee. Her parents were firm in their decision that she apply herself to something useful. I told her it was no use doing anything but following your dreams, but decisions had already been made, and I respected her father's guidance.

We drifted on to other topics. I told her that, during our upcoming company conference, she should do a dance number. She's a fantastic dancer and I asked her to please, please perform a Bollywood number for me.

'Are you crazy? They'll all laugh at me. They'll never speak to me again!'

I gasped again, and trembling, took her hand and dragged her back out on to the terrace. I put my hands on her shoulders and shook her.

'Are they coming back? Are they here right now? Where are they? WHO ARE THEY?' I screamed.

She threw off my hand, 'Chachu, don't be stupid. I mean my friends. My friends will never speak to me again if I perform a Bollywood number. I mean, really...'

But I was really serious. *They* scare me. We are surrounded by *them*. *They* are always watching us, judging us, trying to influence us. Sometimes we know who *they* are. Sometimes, it seems like everyone is against us.

They only thing that *they* do is instil fear. They do not allow us to be who we want to be. And that's damn scary. It's criminal.

On the way out of the office, I told my niece, 'I think it's about time I called the United States Government. They will help us find *them* and eradicate *them*. The US is the best at fighting global crime, wherever and whenever it arises. As Obama said, "These challenges that we face are for real." I think I might give him a call.'

MAKE YOUR PASSION
YOUR PROFESSION

'YOU MAKE HISTORY WHEN YOU HAVE A PASSION
THAT INSPIRES YOU TO WAKE UP EARLIER THAN EVERYONE
ELSE IN THE MORNING, KEEPS YOU
AWAKE LATE AT NIGHT AND FILLS EVERY
MINUTE IN BETWEEN WITH ITS INTENSITY.'

This phrase has been around for centuries. It's a derivative of the Confucius quote: 'Choose a job you love, and you will never have to work a day in your life.'

But I didn't know that, when I first heard Sachin Tendulkar say it. I was sitting in his house, listening to music from *Lagaan* on Sachin's personal stereo. It's an incredible machine, his stereo. It's custom built by a Pune company called Shirke Audio Systems. You won't believe it, but the stereo system takes ten minutes to get warmed up before you can play music on it. It's old-school technology, but as Sachin told me, the sound quality beats any digital sound system.

Anyway, there is no doubt that Sachin is an outstanding athlete. He's also an introvert. A very composed-within-himself sort of human being.

There are quite a few cricketers out there who are driven by greed. Greed to win. Greed for glory. Greed for fame. From all I had seen of him, all the time I had spent in the locker room and on the sidelines with the team, that didn't seem to be the case with Sachin.

I didn't usually disturb him, but, that day, I leaned over and asked him, 'Bro, how do you do it? Stepping out there every day, playing like it's your last game and exceeding even your expectations?'

He looked at me, and all he said, gently, was, 'If you make your passion your profession, then you will not work a single day in your life.' He turned away to adjust the volume on his stereo.

It was so simple a thought. And the more that I applied the thought to his journey, the more impressed I became with him. That's what he had done. Sachin had followed his gut, followed his passion, made it his profession and had given it his all. Keep in mind, when Sachin made this decision twenty-eight years ago, cricket was not a valid career option. It wasn't a reasonable choice of profession in most people's eyes.

But he did it, and he succeeded, because it was truly his passion.

Many of you are working. You've embarked upon a career path. You have a professional title embossed on your visiting card. You look forward to climbing the ladder to the next promotion and the next sequential title.

Think back. Did you choose the career you are pursuing? Did you consciously say to yourself, 'When I graduate from university, I want to be a budget analyst for the Department of Food Processing Industries.'

Be honest. Didn't you want to be a photographer for *National Geographic*? You over there, sitting on the pot instead of writing that project report, wasn't it your dream to be a marine biologist, instead of an industrial engineer? You there, reading this book after stealing it from your brother's room, didn't you want to be an item girl in a Yash Chopra movie?

They convinced you not to, didn't they? 'It's too competitive a field, you'll never get the job.' 'You're not talented enough.' 'It's not a respectable job, honey.' 'You're so good at math and science, please put down that camera and study.'

Of course you listened to them. They were your parents, your teachers, your guidance counsellors, your gurus. Maybe they were right, maybe it wouldn't have been easy earning a living from your passion. Maybe you would have struggled. Maybe you would have had to spend a few years being a steward before getting your big break.

But maybe you could have ended up like Sachin Tendulkar. More than his fame, more than his notoriety, it is that every day of his life, he laces up his shoes, steps out on to the field, and does exactly what he loves to do. The thing that brings him ultimate happiness.

It's never too late to follow your passion. I can vouch for that.

After twenty-five years, I put aside everything that I was doing, and doing very, very well—wheeling and dealing, managing major campaigns, selling ideas to other companies, selling my soul to clients—I put it all aside and did what my gut told me I should do. I wrote this book.

And in writing this book, I learned something that blew my mind. It was never really about 'what' I wanted to be. It was about 'who' I wanted to be.

I didn't want to be a businessman. I never wanted to sell my ideas to someone else.

I realized that all I ever really wanted was credit for being the 'creative genius' that I think I am.

AND THEN? AND THEN AND THEN AND THEN?

'GET LOST TO FIND YOURSELF.'

Ayjaz is driving to Goa after a long week at work. He deserves a little fun in the sun. He's halfway there, when his car breaks down on the highway.

'Son of a bitch!' He kicks the tires. 'I just can't cut a break!'

He flags down a passing car, and the passengers tell him there is a mechanic right up the road. They're happy to give the mechanic the news and send him back to fix the car.

'Sure. Thanks,' Ayjaz says.

Ayjaz smokes five cigarettes by the time the mechanic arrives. 'Fix it fast, I'm late for a meeting.'

Ayjaz always tells people he is late for a meeting, even if he isn't. It makes him look busy and successful.

As he stands there tapping his foot, watching the mechanic dig through his toolbox, he realizes for the first time that he has stopped next to a very beautiful pond.

'Pretty,' Ayjaz thinks briefly before something else catches his eye. There's a man, sitting and leaning against a tree, fishing. He has headphones on his ears and a picnic basket by his side. Even from seeing only half of the back of his head, Ayjaz has this strange feeling that he might know the guy. He knows a lot of people.

In his usual hectic manner, he stomps down the hill, shouting, 'Hey! Hey you!'

The fisherman slowly turns around, sliding his headphones off his ears at the same time. 'Well, I'll be,' he says. 'Ayjaz?'

'Dude, I thought it was you. Haven't seen you since college. What the hell are you doing out here?' Ayjaz bellows.

'I'm fishing, Ayjaz. What are you doing out here?'

'My goddamn car broke down. I knew I shouldn't have traded my Beemer for this piece of shit, but I needed another four-wheel drive. I'm going to friggin' rip the legs off my car guy when I get back. What an ass. Selling me a lemon. I mean, who does he think he's dealing with? I'm not going to be conned like this.'

'Well, if I'm not mistaken, that's Smitesh up there fixing your car. He's good. He should have you back on the road in no time and you can commence with the leg ripping. In the meantime, why don't you sit down?'

Ayjaz sits down, and takes the can of beer that his friend offers him. After a few sips, he asks, 'Really, what do you do out here?'

'I told you, Ayjaz. I fish. I listen to my music. Sometimes, I don't even bring my pole and I just read a book or two.'

'Uh-huh. Right.' Ayjaz lights up another cigarette. 'How many fish do you catch in a day?'

'Oh, some days I don't catch a thing. But there are a lot of fish in this lake. I usually catch about four or five.'

'Really?' Ayjaz takes another deep puff. 'How much do you sell them for?'

'I don't sell them. I take what I can eat, and I release the rest.'

'If you did want to sell them, how much could you sell them for?'

'I don't know. You can buy them for a hundred rupees a kilo in the market.'

'How many ponds like this are there in this district?'

'Thirty, maybe.'

'Huh. If there were a hundred people catching five fish a day, multiplied by thirty ponds...well, that's pretty decent money. You and I should think about getting into business together!'

'And then?'

'Well, we'll form a fishing company.'

'And then?'

'We'll raise some debt, employ some cheap labour, and get this business off the ground.'

'And then?'

'I estimate that we'll show profits in the first year itself.'

'Wow. Really? And then?'

'Dude,' Ayjaz said, lighting up another cigarette, 'within fourteen months, I will list our company on the stock exchange.'

'Oh, shit. Yeah? And then?'

'Our share price will fly. Within a year, we will sell our shares, and make some serious cash!'

'And then?'

'Dude. Uh, then we'll be rich.'

'And then?'

'And then you can retire and do whatever the f?@k retired people do!'

'Like what?'

'Travel. Play golf. Go fishing.'

'Well, you see, Ayjaz... That's exactly what I was doing when you showed up here. I was fishing. Not really sure why I would spend ten years of my life making money so that, when I finally have it, I could come right back here and go fishing. Thanks, Ayjaz. But no thanks.'

'Yeah, fine. Whatever. Suit yourself. I'm going to go see if my car is fixed. I'm late for a meeting.'

YOU'LL BE A GREAT ELEVATOR REPAIRMAN WHEN YOU GROW UP

'F?@K KNOWS WHY OUR EDUCATION SYSTEM TELLS EVERYONE THAT THEY CAN BE A DOCTOR, WHEN THEY'RE BEST SUITED TO BE A CARPENTER.'

The contemporary trend in education is to tell each and every child that they can be a lawyer, a surgeon, an astronaut—they just have to put their mind to it and work hard and they can be really, really smart and make lots and lots of money and live happily ever after. And not only *can* they, but they *have* to.

If you have a class of thirty students, I'd give my left ball that all thirty of them have the mental capacity to become a lawyer. There is no way that all of them have even the basic organizational skills needed to manage their studies to become a doctor. A good percentage of them don't even have the basic math skills to balance their own chequebook or make change for a thirty-seven-rupee purchase—you think they can handle the calculus needed to become an astrophysicist?

Whatever happened to learning a trade? Apprenticeships? Real-life mentors?

Little Smitesh, struggling to stay on top of things in the front row of geometry class, is the son of a mechanic. He grew up in his father's garage, watching his dad fix everything from Enfields to Mercedes SUVs. His father has taught him everything he knows: how to grease up a stuck piston, change a brake pad, replace a gearbox. It comes naturally to Smitesh. He can't tell you the difference between protoplasm and cytoplasm (trick question), but he can tell as soon as a car pulls into the garage that the tensioner pulley needs to be adjusted.

He enjoys working on cars. He's proud of his dad. Nothing would make this boy happier than taking over the garage.

But, since the time he was in the first standard, his teachers have told him, 'Smitesh, if you study hard, if you pass all these tests, then you can be whatever you want to be! Imagine, you don't have to be stuck in a garage all your life, fixing other people's cars. You can be a doctor and save lives, or be a travelling salesman for a pharmaceutical company, or, even (gasp), earn an honest living by serving the government. Reach for the stars, Smitesh!'

If a kid doesn't aspire to be something that society deems 'incredible', then they are already made to feel like a loser.

Why force little Smitesh to believe that his own world is not big enough? Why should he make society proud? Why can't he be happy, making himself proud? Making his dad proud?

Let him be a mechanic. The world needs mechanics. Who's going to fix your f?@king Bentley when it breaks down on Marine Drive on the way to your golf game?

Primary school is not so much about education. It's about teaching discipline. Ideally, schools will have exposed students to a wide variety of professions and areas of further study, but, with so much focus on passing standardized tests and determining IQ, I have a feeling not enough of that is happening.

So, if you are still in the tenth or eleventh grade and were able to sneak a copy of this book from your older cousin, then I just want to tell you that there so many other careers that you can pursue, besides what *they* tell you. Science, engineering, medicine, accounting and law are not the only respectable professions. There are a zillion other options.

Do some research. The best thing is to do some shadowing. If being a dietician sounds interesting, but you're not really sure, then find a dietician and follow him or her around for a few days. India could certainly use some more people who care about what we eat and work towards reducing diabetes. If your heart has been set on becoming a veterinarian since you were a little girl, then spend a week in your local vet's office, and make sure that someday you'll be able to stick your entire arm up a cow's hoo-hoo if the calf gets stuck during delivery.

India still doesn't have a globally recognized fashion designer. Our Bollywood hair and make-up artists can't compete with Hollywood standards. Yet. Oooh, you know what India could really use? Some urban planners! And some soil biotechnology sewage technicians (first developed at IIT Bombay). Any takers?

GET A REAL JOB

Lord Shiva, the man of the house, was out fighting gallant battles on the far side of the universe. Parvati, the woman of the house, wished to take a bath, but needed someone to guard the house and her modesty. Out of the dirt from her body, she lovingly created a young boy and named him Ganesha. She stationed him at the front of the house, with strict instructions not to let anyone enter the house.

Just moments after Parvati had disrobed and slid into the hot, lotus-flower-laden bath, Shiva arrived at the house. The kid took his brief literally and absolutely refused to allow Lord Shiva to enter the house. Being the ultimate rock star that he was, Lord Shiva grew furious with the little boy's impudence. With one quick flick of his wrist, he drew his sword and cut off Ganesha's head.

Hearing the commotion, Parvati came running, barely managing to wrap her towel around herself, and threw herself on the ground beside the fallen boy. 'You vile beast, what have you done to my boy?' she wept.

Shiva panicked, ran out into the forest, cut off the head of the first animal that he found, an elephant, and returned to the house. He attached the head of the elephant to the body of the boy, and Lord Ganesha was reborn. Powerful, and adorable.

Many years later, Brahma came visiting the house. As they chatted over chai, Brahma commented to Parvati that she must be very proud of her boy.

'Eh,' she said.

A little taken aback, Brahma said, 'But he has become a mighty warrior, protector of all, and remover of obstacles. The entire world worships him and exalts his glory. Why are you not happy?'

And Parvati replied, 'I was hoping he would grow up to be an engineer.'

F?@K KNOWS WHY WE DON'T USE THE WORD F?@K MORE OFTEN

'WHAT A F?@KED UP,
F?@KING BEAUTIFUL LIFE THIS IS!'

I love the word 'f?@k'.

It's just such an amazing word. It's so powerful and... versatile.

There's not too much more I can say on this topic, that one of my gurus, Osho, hasn't already said. If you haven't heard his 'f?@k' speech, then you are really missing out. Find it on YouTube—'Osho: Strange Consequences'.

He just about covers it all.

My personal favorite usage of the magic word is: 'F?@k off'.

I don't find it obscene or insulting from any angle. I find it to be a powerful expression of choice. Of my choice, to be precise.

'F?@k off!' stated directly and loudly, indicates my decision that I do not choose you, or what you are offering me at this moment. It also indicates my general pleasure at seeing your face, so you might as well leave, before I punch it.

'Let's f?@k off from here!' whispered to only the closest of friends, clearly indicates my decision that this environment, and its inhabitants, are no longer acceptable.

Two words, containing all the explanation that I should have to give. I can't think of a better way to make myself clear. I can't think of a better release.

The only usage of f?@k that I don't like, is in regards to two people having sex. As in, 'Baby, when we were f?@king the other night, and you handcuffed me to the bedposts...that was really fun, but do you think maybe we should have a "safe word"?'

This may surprise you, but I'm one of those 'I have to be in love, to make love' kind of guys. Physical intimacy is special to me, and I simply cannot f?@k some random...I don't even like to say it. I, ladies and gentlemen, prefer to make love.

Another bonus to using the word f?@k a lot, is that people think you're a bit mental. A rebel against the social norm. A renegade against the system. When you're considered a renegade, you get away with a lot more shit!

'Oh, he did, did he? Well, that doesn't surprise me. He's always been like that, using that terrible language. He doesn't give a rat's backside what we think of him. He's just a big brat.'

If they already think you're a brat, just by your use of language, well then, you have full liberty to live up to that title! Be a brat. Do what you want. Do what makes your heart beat happily. Don't give a shit about what people think of you. Live your life on your terms. And, if *they* don't like it, then tell them to f?@k off!

THE HEALING
POWER OF F?@K

'CHI F?@K! CHI F?@K! CHI F?@K!'

In my life, I have found a further power in the word 'f?@k'—its healing power.

When you train in Tai Chi, and the martial arts, you learn proper breathing for optimum performance. This involves breathing in to your stomach, and saying the word 'chi' as you exhale. By saying this word, you are activating your core, forcing all the breath from your body and calling forth all your strength.

You can feel it yourself. Rest your hand on your stomach, over the belly button, and take a deep breath in. As you exhale, say 'chi'—short and strong. You can feel your lower abdominal muscles tighten and force all the air from your stomach.

Now, keeping your hands on your lower stomach, say 'chi' but before you breathe in again, say 'f?@k'. Can you feel that? The 'chi' activated your core, but the 'f?@k' took the exercise one step further and activated your lower abdominal muscles. Your gut.

We don't focus on, or train our gut at all. Even though, as we discussed earlier, it plays such an important role in helping us find our true direction in life. If we listened more to our gut, and less to our mind, I believe we would all be much better off.

So, in order to activate and strengthen your communication with your gut, today, and today only, I am offering you:

The Shailendra Singh
Chi F?@k Breathing Method

Every time you lift a weight, change a position in Tai Chi, throw an uppercut at the bag, say: 'Chi f?@k!'

Chi f?@k is not only for the gym! It's a great way to start your day! Before you leave the house in the morning, prepare yourself for the challenges of the day by repeating 'Chi f?@k! Chi f?@k! Chi f?@k!' thirty times. You'll notice that you handle stress better and have increased levels of personal calm throughout the day!

Having a stressful day? Chi f?@k also works as a midday meditation!

Shut your laptop, set those papers aside and stand up behind your desk. Close your eyes, and say: 'Chi f?@k! Chi f?@k! Chi f?@k!' Make sure you are exhaling from your stomach, from your core, and you are sure to beat the midday blues!

Girlfriend broke up with you? Mother on your case to get married? No need to be troubled! Turn on your stereo, play your favorite track at full volume and dance around the room shouting 'Chi f?@k! Chi f?@k! Chi f?@k!'

Get your arms involved! Get your legs involved! Flail them around, each moving at its own discretion, release all your stress. Throw your troubles away! 'Chi f?@k! Chi f?@k! Chi f?@k!' Inhale. 'Chi f?@k! Chi f?@k! Chi f?@k!'

With 'Chi f?@k', I guarantee that you will feel immediate results:

- Increased focus!
- Increased ability to remain calm in challenging situations!
- Bigger balls to say 'f?@k off!' to people and things that you do not want!
- A much happier day!

If practiced regularly, with discipline, practitioners have experienced:

- More open communication with the gut!
- Better decision-making capabilities!
- A happier life—living on your own terms!

Because you have been such a great audience, I am offering you Shailendra Singh's Chi F?@k Method absolutely free of charge! It's my gift to you!★

'Chi f?@k' gives me the strength to face whatever life throws at me and makes me really happy. I hope it brings you the same power and joy.

★By accepting this gift, you agree to indemnify the author of any claims and guarantees made in this chapter. There really is no need, because it really works, if you do it right. But still, the author is indemnified.

WHOSE LIFE IS IT ANYWAY?

'LIVE LIFE BY CHANCE, OR BY CHOICE.'

Do I believe in destiny? Do you believe in karma? Do they believe in life after death? Does she believe in luck? F?@k knows what we should believe in.

As I write this, my nephew's best friend just passed away at the age of seventeen. Cancer. Just this morning, my very dear friend, Ajay Gulati, the artist, lost his nephew in a car accident. Nineteen years old. An innocent boy, still waiting to fly, gone. He wasn't driving, he was just along for the ride. He didn't deserve it. He just sat there and had to accept it.

Why do some of us live for a hundred years? And why do some of us die because of diseases or accidents, at a young age? Is it our karma? Is it our past life catching up? Is it our destiny? Or is it just f?@king bad luck?

We spend so much of our life planning for our life. We try to choreograph our journey—the right job, the right promotions, the right husband or wife, the right number of children, the big house, and two dogs—but how often does it work out that way? At any moment, an unknown force can change, alter or divert the course of your life subtly, or not, through doubts, emotions, accidents or incidents.

Nelson Mandela believed in the message of the poem 'Invictus' by the English poet, William Ernest Henley: 'I am the master of my fate, I am the captain of my soul.' Mr Mandela said this after spending twenty-nine years of his life in prison. Was he really in control of his destiny? Did he say to himself one day, 'I have to spend three decades of my life in a dirty jail cell the size of an aircraft bathroom, so that I can take this amazing truth to heart? It will be great training for the day that I am released and become the president of South Africa.'

Did he make those plans? Was he controlling his destiny, or was destiny controlling him?

I'm unable to explain or understand this phenomenon. It totally confuses me. I've travelled the world, met very knowledgeable scientists and gurus, owners of billion-dollar companies, superstars from Bollywood, athletes...none have been able to give me rational answers. Even with all their wisdom and wealth. So I say f?@k it. Maybe we're not meant to know.

Whether it's fate, or not, it really doesn't matter. If it is all in your control then you have to enjoy each and every moment that you are alive, and make the best of it. If it's not in your hands, then you have to enjoy each and every moment that you are alive, because you never know what's in store around the corner. Basically, you just have to enjoy yourself.

DESTINY

My thoughts on destiny are pretty simple. They go something like this:

'Eenie meenie miney mo,
Abhi iske ma chod do.'

If you are an English-only speaker, go ask your Hindi-speaking Indian friend to translate. If you don't have any Indian friends, I'm really amazed that you don't. How have you avoided us? We're everywhere!

Since one out of every six people on the planet is an Indian, I'm sure it won't take you long to find one. Tell them that you want to know more about 'destiny' and recite this to them. Ask them what it means.

Ha ha. Okay, okay. I'll translate for you:

'Eenie, meenie, miney mo,
Now let's f?@k *this* motherf?@ker's life.'

Good things happen to bad people. Bad things happen to good people. There is no logic to it. No pattern. No cause and consequence.

God, Goddess, Allah, Yahweh, Lord (whichever name works for you) pretty much just sits up there and decides luck and tragedy on a whim.

'Okey dokey, er, this boy right there, how old is he?'

'Twelve, God.'

'Right. Let's give him leukaemia. That guy, driving his bike—shift that truck in his way, and let him bash into it. But don't kill him. Give him a spinal injury and let him stay in bed for the rest of his life. This guy, the one who beats his wife and his kids, give him the winning lottery ticket this month.

'This working mother of two, give her arthritis, so that she can barely pick up her kids. This girl, the one who failed her exams, don't stop her from hanging herself from the fan. That politician, who has been embezzling all his constituents' money, which was meant for the temple, let the cops pass over the body he buried in the backyard. Consider that murder "gotten away with".

'Oh, and listen, that Singapore Airlines flight that is flying to Tahiti, how many passengers on board?'

'A total of 246, including the crew, God.'

'Hmmm...hmm...hmmm... Should I crash that into the ocean and kill all of them?'

'You haven't had a good crash in a while, God.'

'True. True. Okay. Do it. Crash it into the ocean. No survivors. But then, don't kill that newborn baby, currently wrapped in her own umbilical cord. Can you unwrap it?'

'Yes, God. Done, God. Baby is unwrapped and currently emerging from its mother's hoo-hoo.'

'Excellent, excellent. Okay, now this guy here...'

Such is life my friends. You have no f?@king clue what's going to hit you next. You have no f?@cking control over some of the biggest, most defining moments of your life. Anything can happen at any time. With no warning. And no reason.

It's nothing more than 'eenie meenie miney mo'...

CONVERSATION WITH GOD

'IT'S OVER?'

Neale Donald Walsch enlightened us with transcripts of his conversations with God. Conversations he held while still here on this earth. They were nice conversations.

I can't be sure, of course, but I have a feeling that when I bite the big one, get my head crushed under a bus or something, and reach the pearly gates, my conversation with God is going to be quite different...

Big G:

'Hey there! It's you! What's up, my child? Sorry I had to crush your head under a bus and all, but...tell me, how much fun did you have down there? Awesome life, huh?'

Me:

'No. Not really, God. I was just about to have a great time when you called me up.'

Big G:

'What do you mean you were *about to*? You're freaking forty-seven years old; what did you do down there for forty-seven years?'

Me:

'Well you know, God, it's like this... From the day that I was born, and first opened my eyes, those two people you gave me to already had a plan for me. The bigger one whispered that he wanted me to grow up to be a doctor, just like him. The more delicate one said that she just wanted me to be happy—as long as it was good grades, a steady job, a beautiful wife and a couple of kids that made me happy.

'I didn't really understand what they were saying so early on, but these two did a great job of bribing me with toys and candy in order to make me learn the things that they thought were good for me. They brought me toys that taught me to fit square blocks into square holes. They brought me LEGO toys to teach me how to create things. They gave me lollipops if I used the potty, or took them away if I bit my brother.

'They read me fables about naughty animals that always eventually got taught a lesson, stories about brothers sticking together to fight armies of enemies, and fairy tales where the prince and the princess always lived happily ever after. When I was five, they put me in school. I surely wouldn't have chosen to go there on my own, but it's not a child's prerogative to decide much of anything.

'We carried on this way for a while. Some candy or a rupee pressed into my palm would stop my crying or make me clean my room. If they said that I should take piano lessons in return for a half hour more of television, I would say, "okay". If they said that if I got higher grades, they would take me to the fair, I would say, "okay". Wash the dishes in return for halwaa? "Sure."

'By the time I had gained consciousness of who I was, I was almost fourteen. I woke up in the morning with nocturnal penile tumescence, also known as "morning wood". When I touched it to figure out what was going on, I ejaculated all over my bed, and then went running to my mother, "What the f?@k just came out of my penis?!" Her discomfort with the discussion that followed taught me to keep further such discoveries to myself.

'From the age of fourteen to sixteen, I was a slave to the

experiments of my own body—how long can I stay hard? (Answer: A long time.) How much of the white stuff can I make in a day? (Answer: A lot.) If I don't get it out, will it get all backed up and choke me? (Answer, gained after a week-long stint of sharing my bed with a visiting cousin: No.)'

Big G:

'That's charming.'

Me:

'Yeah, so, during that time, I was also undergoing "adolescent development"—"the mental transition from childhood to adulthood". I started to hear my own voice in my mind and started desiring things, or to do things, without the promise of candy or to make my parents happy. But as I started to venture after these things—friendships with strange characters, longer cricket matches, shorter homework sessions, closer proximity to girls, adult-content movies—my father would wag his finger and tell me that I would never amount to anything if my grades continued to drop and I hung out with nefarious types. My mother would cry, "I carried him in my womb, I devoted my whole life to him, fed him, made him strong, and this is how he repays me? Arre yaar! What have I done to deserve this?"

'It was hard to believe that this life was meant for me. I was a creation of these two people, who got together—either in a moment of passion, or by accident—made me, and then owned me. I was burdened with the debt of repayment for the gift of life that they had given me. I owed it to them. I was expected to be exactly who they wanted me to be.'

Big G:

'Ah, yes. Expectations. Leave it to you humans to twist a simple survival skill into such a useless complication. You were only supposed to ponder over what was around the next hill, or guess which tree the tiger might jump from to come eat you. You've turned predictive skills into a never-climaxing, mental masturbation.'

Me:

'Yeah, well…it's what life is all about these days. That became clear during my adolescence. I was "expected" to act decently. Be well groomed. Well behaved. Not only expected to go to school every day, even though all I wanted to do was play cricket, but expected to excel! "Why should I?" "Well, my son. That's just what good kids do."

'Till I was twenty-one, I put all my energy into fulfilling their expectations. God forbid (sorry, yaar) my parents' name should get soiled if I didn't graduate with flying f?@king colors. No one cared that I, personally, couldn't give a flying monkey about the things they were teaching me. No one bothered to ask me if I had already identified my best, most promising skills, and in what direction my heart was calling me. I wanted to be an athlete and a creative person, but no one else gave a f?@k.

'I barely passed commerce, went to my father and said, "Listen, papa, I want to be a cricketer." "Kya, paagal hai? (Have you gone mad?)" he asked. "You can't make money as a cricketer. That's not a proper career. You won't amount to anything."

'So, out of fear, I quit my very promising professional cricket career in Scotland and came back to Mumbai to join my brother in the advertising business.'

Big G:

'Aw, that really sucks, beta. You had a dream, and you didn't get to live it. That must have been hard!'

Me:

'Oh? Wait, though. It gets better.

'I worked my ass off to break into the advertising business, learn it, study it, and then excel at it. I have to admit that I did pretty well. I got the hang of it quickly. In no time, I established myself as a dominant force, brought in some huge accounts and started earning some real profits. As soon as the bank account balance started to increase, my parents said I had to get married.

'"What the f?@k are you talking about?" I said, stunned. "I've just started earning money and having fun with it. I've been getting ferociously laid ever since college. Why would I get married?"'

In the West—UK, Europe, America—parents say, "You're sixteen now, f?@k off." And the kids, say "What the f?@k? Why did you bring me into this world if you are just going to kick me out?" But then they also go away to college, get ferociously laid and then don't care any more... But in traditional Indian culture, the pressure is phenomenal. You must get married, you must get married, you must get married. So one day, to stop the ceaseless discussions at the dinner table, you shout: "Goddamnit (sorry, yaar)! Okay, okay. F?@k it! I'll get married!"

Big G:

'My darling son. My poor child. Forced to do so many things you didn't want to do, it's all so sad. But, by this point in your life, you're educated, working and married; your parents must be fully happy; and you must have started enjoying yourself, right?'

Me:

'Ha! That proves you weren't paying attention! I knew there was no way that you could pay attention to all of us, all the time... Omnipresent, my ass...'

Big G:

'Watch it...'

Me:

'Sure, sure. Anyway, before the honeymoon was over—no joke, not even eight months into the marriage—the next expectation

made itself clear. Mom said, "Uh, beta, are you both getting along?"
"Of course. Why?" "Uh, no. Nothing. But...really, you're getting
along?" "Yes, Mama-ji. Everything is fine." "Uh, then, beta... Why
is she not pregnant?" Oh, bloody hell, are you serious?

'So I say, "Shit, Ma, I don't know! Because I don't think we
want a child yet." "No, beta, but that's all wrong. Calculate it—if
you have a child at twenty-five, then when you're forty your child
will be fifteen and you'll be strong enough to carry him on your
shoulders. If you wait too long, you won't be able to run with
him, play with him..." All this logic and experience came flying
at me, and I'm like, "Duuuude. Stop."

'But I gave in, and had the kid.'

Big G:

'Uh-oh.'

Me:

'Yeah... It's a pretty typical story from that point. The first
three years are totally given over to the kid—providing his basic
needs, giving him lots of love and attention, taking care of him
when he falls ill, like kids do, often. Then come the developmental
years, where everything that you show them and teach them
makes a huge impact and you have to give due diligence to
everything you say to them and do with them.

'As they get a bit older, and start to go outside and play
with their friends for hours at a time, you finally get a chance
to reassess where you are in your life.

'At this point I realized how old I had gotten, so quickly. The
hairline was receding, the stomach was protruding. I was forty
and had not done a lot of things that I had meant to do.

'I picked up my pencil and made my F?@k It List: a bicycle
trip from Srinagar to Chennai, sail around the Greek Isles, throw
myself out of a plane, etc. My family saw me hunched over the

table making my list. I started to talk about doing the things on my list, for real. I started researching the right all-terrain bicycle, the best cruises available, where the closest airstrip was for skydiving—Tandem? Or a few lessons and solo hero?

'My family intervened. Said I was having a mid-life crisis. Started whispering to the neighbours about my breakdown.

'*They* do that... *They* scare the f?@k out of you. Tell you you're losing it. Tell you that following your heart is stupid. Naïve. "You should be rational. You know better than this. You have responsibilities. Liabilities. People are looking up to you. You are a known name in society. You have a reputation to protect. You have a child. You have a wife. You have society. You have employees. No. No. No. You must not do all these things that your heart wants. You. Cannot. Jump. Out. Of. A. Plane!"

'"Fine. F?@k it. I won't." I told myself that I'd do it their way for now, but only for a little while longer. "Once I get to f?@king forty-five, woo-hoo, better watch out, f?@kers! I'm going to do whatever the f?@k I want! And no one is going to stop me!"'

Big G:

'Finally! It's about time!'

Me:

'Yeah, well. Not so fast, big guy. As soon as you hit forty-five —Hello! Life starts to collect its toll. Diabetes, blood pressure, heart problems, arthritis, nerve attacks, some f?@king shit or the other hits you. It's not even necessarily because of your age, but more because you have not lived your life up until now. You haven't flown. Your juices, your breath, your blood has not flown like it should through your body. You have been under so much stress because, for so long, you have been someone you are not.

'I guess after forty-five years of pretending to be someone else, you deserve to fall ill. It's only logical. In my opinion, after forty-five years of pretending, of suppressing your dreams and living on someone else's terms, you *should* die. Just f?@king kick the bucket.'

Big G:

(Clears throat)

Me:

'Ha ha. Yeah, well, so. I guess that's why I'm here.'

Big G:

'F?@k, man! That's hectic. I gave you a sweet, simple life to live, and you've made a mess of it.'

Me:

'F?@king hectic, for sure. I did my best. You go give it a try, God! See if you can do better.'

Big G:

'No thanks, my child.'

Me:

'Okay, better yet, big dude, could you give me another try? Give me another two years, and I promise you that I will live all my forty-eight years in those two years!'

Big G:

'Uh, no can do. But we do have a fantastic bar and spa up here. You are welcome to finally enjoy yourself, be yourself, here. Or you can keep wandering around, cribbing about the life you led down there. Up to you.'

Me:

'Well, heck… I guess if it's possible to be dying all the while that you are alive, it's possible to be living while you are dead, right?'

Big G:

'F?@k knows, my son!'

Me:

'Does the bar stock Moët Rose?'

LIFE

'F?@K KNOWS WHY YOU NEED DEATH,
TO MAKE YOU LIVE.'

Visualize a hand full of sand. As you hold the sand in your palm, it starts to trickle gently through your fingers. Slowly, but steadily, it slides quietly away.

If you squeeze your fist, in order to hold on to the sand longer, it only forces the sand out faster. It finds any crack, any break in the seal, to escape. Whether you hold it lightly and let gravity work on each and every grain, or squeeze it and force it out quicker, in one way or the other, the sand is going to find a way out.

That is life. It is a diminishing process. Each day you live, you are one day closer to death. You think you are going to live forever, especially if you are still under thirty. But that's obviously not true. So with each passing breath, each passing morning, day, night, you are heading towards the end of your story.

Only in truly accepting that one day you are going to die does the purpose of life, the celebration of life, become more significant. You are going to die. Now start living like you mean it.

At St Xavier's High School, there was a Parsi boy whom I studied with from the fourth standard until the tenth. He was a little bit mad, sweetly cracked. He always brought his lunch to school in colour-coded Tupperware containers of just the perfect size. He was very clinical in his thinking and anal in his actions.

Most people found him annoying, but I found him damn funny.

After graduation, I lost track of him, but often wondered about him. One day, fifteen years later, I stopped into Snowman's to buy a milkshake. Snowman's was a very popular, small milkshake parlour near Breach Candy Hospital. It was eventually turned into a small restaurant called 'The Right Place'. Now it's a Mad Over Donuts.

But that day, when I went for a chocolate milkshake, there he was, having already ordered the same thing.

'Duuude! Long time. What's up?' I said.

'Whoa, Shailu! Not much, man! Long time indeed!' he said. 'I just came to Breach Candy to donate some blood. My mother's not well. She's in need of B-positive blood.'

I won't lie to you. I'm pretty sure I'm B-positive, but I am so petrified of hospitals and needles that I didn't volunteer or let him know that I could be a potential donor. Since I was meeting him after so long, though, and wanted to catch up, I told him that I would go with him to visit his mother.

When we reached Breach Candy Hospital, I said I would wait outside, while he went to give blood. He said, 'Don't worry, this is the new wing of the hospital. It doesn't smell like a hospital or anything!' He lured me in with some glucose biscuits and some coffee and we sat on a bench just outside the lab.

Obviously, when you donate blood, they run thorough evaluations and check to make sure your blood is healthy and suitable for donation. It's a tricky deal, mixing people's bodily fluids together. During the thirty-minute wait for the test results, we chatted about life.

'How the f?@k are you, dude? What are you up to?' I asked him.

'I'm married. I have two kids,' he answered.

'Are you serious? Who the f?@k would marry you?'

'Ha. Don't worry, she's just like me. A Parsi.'

'You're going to become extinct soon, you know? You only marry each other, hang with each other. Can't be good for the lineage.'

We had a great time catching up. He was working in a bank. Very content with his situation and place in life. Just worried about his mother.

Then the nurse came out. She called him inside for the test results. I had no intention of leaving the bench, but he said, 'Come, come, you haven't told me about you.'

The nurse had a teeny tiny little room and a no-nonsense attitude. She cut right to the chase. 'Your blood is fine and all, but we can't give it to your mother. There's a small issue with it.'

F?@k knows why, but I was the one who asked, 'Why, what's wrong with it?'

The nurse looked at me, and then back at him. Then back at me. To him, she said, 'Could you please leave the room and let me speak to your friend?'

We both reacted, like, 'Uh, what are you saying? It's his/my blood. Talk to him/me.'

To him, she said, 'Sir, if you really don't mind, just let me consult with your friend before I speak with you.'

I said, 'I just popped in from across the street. This is no business of mine.'

'I'd be much happier talking to you first, sir. Privately,' she insisted.

Okay, whatever. My friend sheepishly stepped outside, a puzzled expression on his brow. As soon as the door clicked closed, the nurse said, 'He's HIV-positive. I can't give the blood to his mother.'

'What the… What are you saying? That can't be right. He's got a wife and two kids…'

'Yeah, that's a serious situation that you need to tackle, but a bit later. For now, we need to find blood for his mother. She's in the ICU, and I can't give her this blood. So, get me *clean*'—she spoke that word very pointedly—'clean B-positive blood for his mother, now. Then, it's your prerogative to tell him that he's HIV-positive, or hold your peace, so that he doesn't fall apart while his mother needs him most.'

'F?@k.'

F?@k, f?@k, f?@k. Was this really happening? I stepped outside. Instinct kicked in, I lied to my friend. Working in advertising has made me a pretty decent liar. I told him that his blood count was not high enough to be able to use, due to a slightly weakened immune system, or some crap like that. I said that we would have to go out and find donors for his mother.

To calm him down, I promised that I would make some calls and get some people there. I did, and within fifteen minutes, friends were stopping in to donate blood. One of those friends, an Iranian boy, was a mutual friend from our school days. I explained the situation to Friend Number Two. Without hesitation, he said that I had to tell Friend Number One the truth.

'No f?@king way!' I said. 'Who am I to just wander into this guy's life and destroy it on the same day? No way.'

But Friend Number Two was adamant. 'You have to tell him, Shailu. He needs to know. And he needs to know he is putting his wife and kids at risk. You have to tell him.'

I just didn't have the guts to do it. I didn't have the balls to tell Friend Number One that he was…'unclean'. Friend Number Two wouldn't back down. So, I walked away from the hospital, without saying goodbye.

Friend Number Two told him that day. I don't know whether he was stronger, or more stupid. I didn't ever have the courage to see Friend Number One again. I heard that six months later, his mother passed away. Six years later, he passed away. He left behind his wife and two kids. Left them behind, and died of AIDS.

People die of many things—leukaemia, cancer, AIDS. People die from influenza. People die from diarrhoea, for Christ's sake. It's not about the disease. The lesson for me was that in a split second, your whole concept of life can be destroyed.

From working hard in a bank, falling in love with his wife, having two children, and having many fruitful years ahead to enjoy what he had built...boom! He gets the news. His universe falls apart. And death hunts him down.

F?@k knows when it will find us. But it will.

If it finds you tomorrow, will you die happy? Will you go, content that you made the most of the time you were given?

STAYING ALIVE

'F?@K KNOWS WHY WE VALUE THE PACKAGING
MORE THAN THE PRODUCT.'

I have always had a penchant for celebrating life. I have always, in my own way, given thanks for what I have. But the experience with my Parsi friend in Breach Candy Hospital struck so deep into my core, that from then on, each morning, when I open my eyes, I give thanks for the opportunity to live another day.

Why should it have hit me so deeply? He wasn't my best friend. He wasn't a family member. I hadn't seen him for fifteen years, for Christ's sake!

Maybe because of exactly those things—the experience was close enough to affect me, but distant enough that I could, to some extent, remain objective—did it hit me so hard. For an instant, his life crossed paths with mine. He came back into my life. And in the very next instant, I was told that he was on his way out.

Emotionally, I was bewildered. Professionally, the experience began to change the intent of my work, the purpose of my work. I began to try, in my own way, each and every day, to make a difference.

I guess I realized that, at the end of day, I wanted my work to create more than profits. When the time for me to leave this world came, I wanted to leave behind more than balance sheets, bank accounts and receipts.

...arted doing everything a bit differently. With a deeper purpose. This is something that very few people around me noticed. To this day, no one—including my brother (also my business partner), my mother, my friends—really understands that my work is much more than just 'doing business'.

The very first feature film I ever produced, *Pyaar Mein Kabhi Kabhi* (Sometimes in Love), I made with 190 debutants. Everyone who acted in that film, made that film—creative directors, hairstylists, make-up artists, music directors—was a debutant. A fresh face.

No one in Bollywood likes to take a risk by banking on new talent. Indians, in general, don't like to take risks. They prefer a sure shot. A debutant is always launched in a film starring across a bankable superstar.

There were, and are, so many talented people in India, just waiting for a break. I took the punt. It certainly gives me a sense of pride to know that, out of those 190 debutants, sixty of them are now award winners—musicians, background score actors, superstars in the industry. Whether they acknowledge it or not, I know that Percept and I had the balls to make a movie that launched so much fresh talent in one shot.

Having said that, what was the essence of *Pyaar Mein Kabhi Kabhi*?

To date, nobody has really picked up on the true meaning of the film. What I would insist is the fundamental crux of the movie, the reason I made the movie, is usually only mentioned in passing in the last sentence of the plot summary on Wikipedia or IMDB.

The movie is centred on four friends who embark upon a musical journey. In remaining true to their hearts and creating their own music, they are captaining their own lives. There are many parallel stories—the boy loves the girl, but the girl loves the other boy, who overlooks her for a sexpot who takes him for a ride—and many life lessons are learned. But deep into their journey, one of the friends finds out that he is HIV-positive.

HIV and AIDS were rarely touched upon in Bollywood in 1999. No one wanted to talk about it. Not just in Bollywood, but in the general public as well. Even today, in India, most diseases, illnesses and the people who have them, are taboo. The sick are to be avoided and feared. Especially those with AIDS. The ailment is not to be discussed and sympathy is not to be shown.

There are many who believe illness and disease are inflicted upon people because of their bad karma. What bullshit. It could be my fate, or hers, or his, or yours tomorrow, to fall ill. Would you believe the same for yourself—that you deserved to fall ill? That it was punishment for something bad you did in the past? Wouldn't you want just the most basic human sympathy and understanding?

For the first time in India, through *Pyaar Mein Kabhi Kabhi*, I highlighted some of the most severe misconceptions about HIV and AIDS. I showed that you can touch an HIV-patient without getting infected, a stigma attached to HIV at the time. I showed that it was not a 'gay epidemic', and that the disease could be spread by a number of different means. These were powerful public service messages, and certainly more than the Ministry of Health was doing at the time.

In the second half of the movie, unlike my own hasty retreat from Breach Candy Hospital, his friends don't abandon their HIV-afflicted buddy. They do not blame him. They don't fear him. They support him. They stick together, shift their purpose in life and hold a concert to raise money for his treatment.

At the climax of the movie, when they are all up on stage

performing their breakthrough track, the lyrics say: 'It's time to celebrate life, it's time to unite in life, time to understand its significance.' I still get goosies when I hear that song.

The opening weekend of the movie was house full, all over the country. Friday, Saturday, Sunday were packed. But as word spread that there was a moral to the movie, a deeper meaning, ticket sales dropped. The audience wasn't able to turn to their friends and say: 'The movie was fantastic, and you know, I learned something about HIV/AIDS.'

The HIV angle just wasn't feasible to discuss yet. Society is shallow. People don't really care about deeper meanings. They want the glitz and glamour of a perfect love story, and a happy ending. No one really wants to acknowledge the darker side of life.

The industry hype and hysteria over the film was phenomenal, however.

A few years passed, and in 2004, I made another movie on the cause of HIV. *Phir Milenge* starred India's A-list actors, Shilpa Shetty, Salman Khan and Abhishek Bachchan and, this time, the whole movie revolved around the disease and its consequences.

Not coincidentally, Tamanna (Shilpa Shetty) learns that she is HIV-positive after she donates blood at her local hospital to replace the blood used in her sister's transfusion.

Again, the movie didn't do exceptionally well at the box office, but it certainly caught the attention of the industry and media. In recognition of producing India's first movie about HIV/AIDS, I was presented with the Staying Alive Award from MTV.

It was a really huge moment for me, receiving that award. It was a highly emotional moment—the culmination of so many lessons, so much dedication, hard work and so many good intentions.

It was the ultimate award of the night, presented by Kamal

Hassan, South India's Number One Actor, and Alanis Morrisette, Rock Goddess. When they called my name, the 5,000-strong MTV generation went mad with excitement, still full of energy at the end of the night.

Shilpa Shetty took my arm, and we walked up on to the stage. I wasn't so great at public speaking back then. Fifty million appearances on *Times Now* with Arnab Goswami have changed that, but, back then, I had prepared my speech and kept it neatly folded in my jacket pocket.

Once I reached the podium, though, and faced the crowd, I couldn't take the paper out. I felt a tug deep in my gut. Realizing there was a transmission coming in from my heart, I closed my eyes for one second and listened.

My heart told me that this moment wasn't about the award in my hand. It was about completing the circle. It was about finishing the job that I had set out to do.

Shouting into the mic, over the maddening din of the crowd, I said to them, 'Ladies and gentlemen, will you all do me a favour? Can you please be silent, just for a moment.'

What was I doing? The MTV grind platform was whistling and shouting, the MTV mosh pit on the other side was screaming: 'Shilpa! Shilpa!' Kamal Hassan, Shilpa, and friggin' Alanis Morrisette were all clapping for me, for the movie. And I was asking all of them to quieten down. Who the f?@k does that?

But they all went quiet.

'Now, do me another favour. All of us together, let's take a long, deep breath.' They started slowly, hesitantly, but eventually I heard the entire crowd take in a deep breath.

'Now, let's all release that breath together.' A tremendous whooshing sound traversed the auditorium.

'You have just celebrated the biggest moment of your life.

You have celebrated the fact that you are alive. Never take this life for granted. Enjoy the moment that you have. It's here. You're here. You're breathing. *That* is worth celebrating. *Now,* you f?@king clap!'

And they did. Even louder than before.

EVENTUALLY, IT HITS
CLOSER TO HOME

'PRESENT IS THE PAST. AND FUTURE UNKNOWN.'

My father was happy, healthy, physically fit. An elegant man—6'2" with shining silver hair. Then, he was diagnosed with lung cancer.

He had come to my brother and me, saying that he was having appetite problems. Wasn't feeling too great, not eating well. We took him for a few basic tests, but they were all clear. The lack of appetite persisted. One of our doctors suggested that maybe we should try a more specific oncology test. 'Oncology, isn't that for cancer?' We were told it wouldn't hurt to just rule it out.

So, one morning, Harry and I casually took him to the oncologist. There was no chance that he could have something so seriously wrong with him. He was such a strong man. He was indestructible. He was our Superman. We were just following protocol.

Even though my brother and father were sitting in the waiting room with me, the oncologist, Dr Desphande, asked me to come into his office to discuss the test results. I don't know why I am always the one to get the bad news.

'You must look after your dad.'

'We do! Actually, he looks after us. He's too strong.'

'Yeah, but, you need to look after him now. He's only got four months left to live.'

'What's that now?'

'Yeah, he's only got four months left. He's in the fourth stage of lung cancer.'

'Uh...fourth stage? What happened to stages one, two and three?'

'Sometimes the internal organs are so strong, that they can fight the disease themselves without you ever knowing it's happening.'

'So you are saying that my father has four months left to live on this planet?'

'Yeah.'

I laughed. 'Are you for real? What if that's unacceptable?'

'Well, you can speak to Dr Advani. He's the best in Asia. He's in Jaslok Hospital, which is the only nuclear ward around, but you must approach him immediately. He'll start working on the chemo, but I have to be honest with you—it's really only downhill from here. Your father has reached the stage where nothing can be done for him. It's really the end of the line.'

It was a very practical conversation. My heart was starting to shatter into little pieces, but I knew it wasn't the time, nor the place to fall apart. I put on my poker face and left his office.

I walked out and told Harry and dad, 'Let's go, it's all done.'

We dropped dad off at home, and I followed Harry into his office. I stood there, not sure what to say. Go with the obvious, I guess. 'Bro, dad's got four months to live.'

I was ready to start crying my balls off, but my brother is very strong. And very practical. Pragmatic. He immediately started flipping through his mental Rolodex, figuring out which doctors we could call, what treatments we could line up. He was ready for action. Ready to solve the problem. Get it fixed. He led the charge.

Dad was the strongest of all, though. He went through twenty-one chemotherapy sessions, which was unheard of. And after each chemo, he would still come to office.

Smack in the middle of all this, surely due to the sadness in my heart, I had a neurological nerve problem in my leg. I was bedridden for fourteen days. They put a hospital bed in my house. For twenty-three-and-a-half hours a day, I couldn't move from a flat bed. It sucked. The only person who visited me each and every day was my father. He was going through chemo, but he was the only one who came to see me.

He used to walk into my makeshift hospital room wearing an elegant English beret and a blazer, and sit and chat with me. I got better, my father got worse.

As a last resort, the doctors offered us an experimental nuclear test. It was a one in a million chance, but hey, f?@k knows what's possible in this world! It didn't work, but, as part of the testing process, he had to fill out a questionnaire. To this day, I'm not really sure about the diagnostic benefit of the survey, but they asked him all sorts of questions about life. One of the questions was, 'What is the happiest moment of your life?'

His answer was, 'When I talk to my youngest son. He gives me wisdom in a manner that makes me laugh, but with a full understanding of the meaning of what he is saying.'

For me, that was the ultimate. The end of the road. Hearing that, from my father, my mentor, my reason for living...there was nothing else left for me. Mission accomplished. I was ready to check out. I was ready to go with him.

YOU HEAR ABOUT TSUNAMI?

'LIFE IS PAINFUL.
YOU JUST HAVE TO PLAY IT THROUGH.'

When my father died of lung cancer, I wanted to die too. I seriously thought about killing myself. I have never admitted this to anyone. F?@k knows why I am sharing it with you.

I'm generally a very optimistic person. A 'life enthusiast', if you will. I believe that life is a very precious gift, and that every moment should be cherished and lived to its fullest potential.

But my father was my entire life. He was my guru. My teacher. My reason for being. I lived to learn from him, make him proud, keep him smiling. When he left, I was without reason. Directionless. I had no desire to carry on.

I felt justified in giving up, justified to take my own life. I felt that I was the most forlorn person on this planet. I thought there was nothing worse that could happen to someone than losing the one person that they loved most in the world. What *could* possibly be worse?

As I asked that question, in the darkest hour of the night, it struck me that it wasn't rhetorical. I really wanted to know. Life gave me an answer.

To help cheer me up, my best buddy at the time, Asif Khan, decided to take me on an ecological adventure in Thailand. Yes, sand and sea, birds and fish, sunsets and sunrises. Not Patpong, ladyboys and cheap sex.

We stayed in Phuket and did all the things that tourists do. Well, what wealthy tourists do. Drank champagne next to the five-star resort's infinity pool. Had two-hour Thai massages. Took long walks on the beach. Hired a private yacht for just the two of us. (Just for the record, Asif is a good-looking guy, bald and waxes his chest, but we are not lovers.)

So, we hired this yacht, complete with a local captain and his assistant to take us to Koh Phi Phi Island. It's the island where the movie *The Beach* was filmed.

It really is as beautiful as it looks in the movie. Pure, virgin beaches. Green jungle. Crystal clear, deep blue water. We snorkelled on the reefs, watched the fish, poked the giant sea slugs and collected pretty shells. We lay in the sand and dried off in the sunshine. It was paradise. I thought about my father a lot. I wished he could have seen it.

When we boarded the boat to head back to the mainland, the skies were a clear blue, the ocean was calm and there was a gentle, salty breeze blowing. As he offered us some local fruit, the captain mumbled something about the possibility of hitting a small patch of bad weather. We were just peeling our second banana when the sky began to turn dark grey and it began to drizzle.

I swear to God, no lie, within sixty seconds we were in the middle of a massive storm. The skies opened up. Thunder! Lightning! The waves got bigger and meaner! Just like in the movies. It was a perfect storm. I'm not exaggerating. Call Asif, he'll tell you: +91 9821328616. I was George Clooney. Asif was Mark Wahlberg. And we were both going down with the ship.

We were bashed and battered, flipped and f?@ked, for the

next twenty minutes. The boat almost turned turtle a few times, before the captain asked us to tie a rope around our waists, and then tie the other end to the boat. We did not know if we were going to make it out alive. It occurred to me that maybe this was life giving me what I wanted—to be with my father again.

But, as quickly as it came, the clouds blew past, the sunshine returned and we were again gliding on a calm sea. We were shell-shocked for a few minutes. There was nothing but a single grey cloud rapidly disappearing into the distance to prove that the storm had happened. Unf?@kingbelievable.

When the adrenaline started to wear off, the panic set in. I jumped up to find the captain. I forgot that I was still tied to the boat and when the rope caught, I jackknifed on to my face. After I picked myself up and untied the rope, I ran to the captain and shouted, 'What the f?@k was that? You said a small storm? What the f?@k were you thinking? Were you trying to kill us?' There was still some adrenaline left in my veins and I was mad as hell.

The captain looked at me with calm, grey eyes, and responded slowly, 'Why you shout with so much anger?'

I was taken aback. He wasn't reacting to my aggression. His question penetrated deeper.

He turned the key, shutting off the engine, and left the boat adrift in the open sea. 'You, good man. Let me tell you my story.'

He flipped open the glove box under the windshield, and pulled out a much-handled photograph. It was a family portrait, his mother, wife and five children posed stiffly, but lovingly. His kids were aged between four and fourteen. They all looked very happy.

'You hear about tsunami last year in Thailand, no?' he asked.

'Of course,' I answered.

'Look there.'

I turned my gaze to follow his outstretched arm.

'What do you see?' he asked.

'I see...sea.'

'In the sea, you see a small bump? A hill?'

'Oh, yeah, I do. It's hard to see, but I see it.'

He dropped his arm, but continued to stare at the small hill of sand. 'That was my village. Three thousand people live in my village. Last year, tsunami came. Wipe away whole village. Take away all my six reasons to live.'

I couldn't say anything. What can you say to something like that?

'That was six month ago,' he said softly, still staring out over the ocean.

Finally, I stammered, 'But, h-how can you come back on to the sea?'

The captain sighed. 'I don't know what else to do. Was it nature? Was it angry sea? Was it destiny? Was it my karma? I don't know what I did to deserve to lose everybody. I was very angry for some time. But what was the point? It brought no answers.'

So many things were running through my mind. I couldn't fathom how he was coping. Where did he find the strength? I couldn't understand why the Almighty of the universe had brought such pain to such a gentle human being. How could life be so cruel? But, most of all, how was this man surviving it?

'I don't think I will ever know answer of why,' he said. 'All I know is, if my family were here, they would wish me where I love to be. At sea. So I come. It is what I know.'

He could still feel the love of his family for him, and his love for them made him press on. I still had my wife, my son, my mother...a lot of family that loved me; and a lot of love left to give my family and my friends.

My suicidal thoughts ended that day. If that captain could lose everyone he loved and still be able to find his peace in this world, how could I cry for myself?

Life sure does have a way of humbling the spirit.

TWO AND A HALF FRIENDS

'TO GET TO THE TOP IS TOUGH. TO STAY THERE, EVEN TOUGHER.
THE WAY DOWN IS AMAZING,
AS THERE IS NO TOP AT THE BOTTOM.'

'LET'S BE GOOD FRIENDS... NOW, F?@K OFF!'

When you are going uphill, you have a thousand friends. No shortage of buddies to grab a drink with after work, dance on the $8,000 Versace leather couch, hit the city streets in the custom-built, champagne-bar-on-wheels Mercedes. When you're on your way up, there are a lot of people to cheer on the effort in the hope of sharing in the spoils.

When you've reached the top, another thousand friends welcome you to the club. They invite you to every party, stop by in the middle of the night to ask your kitchen for chicken sausages and help themselves to the bottle of 1926 Macallan Fine and Rare that you were saving to gift to your son on his wedding day. Life is good. Expensive, but good.

When you start on the inevitable roll back downhill—global recession wipes out your fortune, the lead actor of the movie you invested most of your savings in totally scams you and makes sure your movie bombs, you forget to sign the pre-nup on your third marriage to that Slovenian supermodel—when you come crashing down from your pinnacle, I guarantee that you will find exactly two and a half friends by your side.

I learned this poignant lesson during my close call with death. When I was hospitalized for the heart attack, I went through a lot of emotions and anguish. One half of me almost relished the fact that I might soon be back by my father's side. The other half of me was shit scared to give up this life. There were still so many things left to do on my F?@k It List.

Before the illness, I was at my peak. The media kept track of me. Clients wanted to do business with me so that they could party with me. I was a very popular guy. I had two thousand friends. I had over a thousand employees, most of whom had been with the company for over a decade. Guess how many of those 'friends' came to visit me at the hospital.

Lying there in the hospital bed, staring at the ceiling, trying not to notice the IVs and tubes and needles and monitors, I was sure that five hundred people would come and visit me. Five hundred people would wonder why I missed two days in a row at work, something I had never, ever done before. Five hundred people would want to give me their good wishes, bring me bouquets of flowers, and come tell me, 'Don't be worried, you're going to be just fine.'

What was your guess of how many people came to visit me? Good guess. I'll tell you how many came. Five. Five people came to visit me.

Only one of them brought flowers.

When I finally went back to work one week later, on a Monday morning, five hundred people came to see me. They said that they all guessed that I would bounce back quickly, that I looked strong, and they were happy I didn't die. But I wasn't moved. I'm not a dumb guy. They only came to meet me because they needed something from me. Some work was pending, and they were relieved that I was there to sign it, fix it, approve it or close it.

They weren't there when I needed them. They didn't come to the hospital to see if they could donate blood for me. Now that I was back at work, the motherf?@kers were there to suck some more of my blood!

'Heard you were unwell. How are you feeling now? You're looking good, dude. Good, good. So, about that thing we were discussing, can we meet on Tuesday for it?'

'Hey, boss, how are you feeling? Crazy thing, huh? Hits you just like that... So, I was wondering if you could sign off on that budget for me?'

'Hey. You're back, where were you? Vacation? No? Oh. Anyway, about that thing...'

Bloodsucking bastards.

If I had actually died, mind you, there would have been five thousand people at my funeral. Being reasonably famous, as I was, at least in Mumbai, my funeral would have been decently high profile. A place to be seen. A 'must-attend soiree'.

'Hey, dude, are you going to Shail's funeral?'

'Yeah, man. He was a cool dude.'

'Even I'm going! Around ten, ten-thirty?'

'Yeah, we'll all be there. Hey listen, after that, you want to stop in for the champagne brunch at Zoe Cafe?'

'Sure, man! All-you-can-drink champagne? Woo-hoo!'

Five thousand people would have come to my funeral back in those days. Five hundred thought it prudent to lay their good wishes on my desk. Five actually came to the hospital to hold my hand and tell me, when I needed it most, that everything was going to be okay.

I thought even deeper about this. Of those five friends who came to visit me, which of them did I actually want, with all my heart, to be there beside me? Whom would I choose to hold my hand in the darkest moments of my life? And whom would I call in the most glorious moments of my life?

For sure, I would want my best friend of two decades to be there. No question about it. That's one.

Without a doubt, I would want my other best friend by my side. I had met him more recently, but we already had a super-strong, unconditional bond. Like we had known each other in many previous past lives. That's two.

And then...ummm... Maybe this other guy. But... I'm not really sure, though. If I really think about it... I guess not. He's great, but...could I make it by without him? Probably. Oh! You know who? I would call this other guy. We party all the time, but...actually, when it comes to serious stuff... Yeah, I'm not totally sure...

That's two and a half people. More than two people, but not a definite three. Two and a half people who would give up anything to be by your side, and who you would actually want to give up everything to be by your side. People who love you unconditionally. That's it.

Friends will come and go in times of sickness and health, for richer or poorer, for better or worse, but those two and a half will be there for you, always. Who are your two and a half friends? And have you told them lately, how much they mean to you?

True friends are hard to come by. When you find them, keep them close. F?@k knows when you'll need someone to hold your hand, and tell you that everything is going to be all right.

JUST A LITTLE MORE HUMILITY, PLEASE

'SOMETIMES YOU GAIN TO LOSE AND
SOMETIMES YOU LOSE TO GAIN.'

We humans like to think of ourselves as the most intelligent of all earth's creatures. We can use tools, we can use tools to make other tools. We have language, compassion and reasoning skills. But one thing we still don't have a good grasp on, is foresight. Life usually has to smack us in the face and bash us around a bit, before we are ready to learn a lesson. We usually have to have an accident, or experience an incident, before we really understand.

When you are young, the lesson usually has to be intensely physical for it to sink in. Even though your mother told you time and again not to touch the tea kettle, you somehow didn't get it. You went and touched the kettle and burnt off the first two layers of skin on your fingers. Smelled fantastic. But I bet you didn't touch the kettle again.

As you grow older, the lessons get more intensely emotional. You will not understand death, until someone you love dies. You will not understand financial loss, until you lose every f?@king penny in your bank account. You will not understand what 'don't drink and drive' means until you finish a bottle of vodka, get behind the wheel, and hit a child on the road.

You usually won't *know*, until it happens to you. The older and the wiser can share their stories and give you advice. They hope that maybe you can avoid a few of the same mistakes, avoid just a bit of the pain. But, for the most part, you won't learn. You'll have to feel it for yourself.

It is possible, however, to feel a bit of it, without suffering all of it. A good movie can really touch you deep inside and make you feel something strongly, as if it is actually happening to you. You can get lost in a great book and lose yourself in space and time. An incredible painting can bring forth emotions that you have no chance of hiding.

Obviously, we all prefer the good things in life. We avoid exposure to the 'bad things' as much as possible. We stash away our lepers in faraway colonies, we turn away from the beggars carrying limp, lifeless babies in the hot sun. In the grocery store, we get our meat de-boned, filleted, and wrapped individually in crystal clear Saran wrap. It doesn't even look like it was once alive. You don't even have to remember that something died in order to feed you.

We don't like to see the bad stuff. But, just like you can only appreciate the sunlight because you have lived through the night, you will only truly understand the blessings that you have when you catch a glimpse of those who don't.

Here's my humble suggestion. The next time you are feeling too cool—Daddy just bought you a new convertible, you just won the businessman-of-the-year award, made a million bucks off a stock market scam—or, whenever you are feeling like you just can't cut a break—your project lost its sponsor, you caught your girlfriend cheating with your best friend, and she gave you an STD—balance it all out with a little humility.

Take a stroll through the Tata Memorial Hospital, or go to the Massena Memorial Hospital in Mumbai. Just spend fifteen minutes walking the corridors of these two hospitals. You don't have to talk to anyone. You don't have to stay there for hours. You don't have to do anything. Just walk. Listen. And feel.

I guarantee that after a brief stroll, you will walk out of the hospital valuing what you have, more than on any other day of your life.

As I write this chapter, I get a phone call. A friend of mine, forty-three years old, has lost his memory to a viral infection. He's been in the hospital for a month, in and out of consciousness. He doesn't really recognize any of his family who come to visit him, but he appreciates their company in the sterile, grey hospital room.

'He's better now, although I can't guarantee that he'll know who you are. His entire life's journey has been wiped away. His accomplishments, his triumphs, our family memories…it's all gone. Won't you come visit him?' his wife asks.

As I climb into the car to go visit him the next morning, I get another call. 'Your cousin just lost both of his parents in a car crash,' they tell me. My cousin is only sixteen years old. Now, he's sixteen and parentless. Goddamn it.

Same day—I am not kidding, when the shit hits the fan, it f?@king explodes!—I get another call. My best friend's son has poked himself in the eye. He was running around with some sort of stupid pointy toy, tripped and fell right on top of it. He will be partially blind forever. He's seven years old.

Shit, dude.

Today, if you are breathing, can see with your eyes, hear through your ears, eat with your mouth, write with your hands, walk on your legs, then you are goddamn blessed. If you are healthy, you are wealthier than any billionaire, and you better celebrate that. Celebrate now, my friend. Not tomorrow.

I keep telling you the same thing. Are you listening?

F?@k knows what is going to happen tomorrow. There might be no tomorrow.

F?@K KNOWS WHY...

1945-1981

Bob Marley died of cancer at the age of thirty-six, just as his music, voice and message were making the world stand up and listen.

1869-1948

Mahatma Gandhi was shot dead at seventy-eight, after a lifetime of preaching non-violence.

1961-1997

Princess Diana died in a car accident at the age of thirty-six, just when she was finally finding her own happiness.

1940-1973

Bruce Lee died at the age of thirty-two from an allergic reaction to a common painkiller, after he had spent his whole life perfecting his body and his craft.

1965-1993

Brandon Lee was accidentally shot dead at twenty-eight years of age, seventeen days before he was to be married, while following in his father's footsteps.

1955-2011

Steve Jobs died of cancer at fifty-six, when he had so much more innovation to share.

1979-2001

Aaliyah died in a plane crash at twenty-two years of age, cutting short a remarkable career before it even began.

1998-2012

Taruni Sachdev died at age fourteen in a plane crash in Nepal, before even having a chance to show the world what she could do.

1933-1960

Madhubala was born with a hole in her heart and only lived until thirty-six.

1929-1968

Martin Luther King Jr was shot dead at age thirty-nine, after working for years to advance civil rights through non-violent civil disobedience.

1955-

Dawood Ibrahim, third on the Forbes' World's 10 Most Wanted List of 2011, is still alive.

1938-

Bernard Madoff, Ponzi schemer of the largest financial fraud in history, is still alive.

1954-

Joaquìn Guzmàn Loera, aka El Chapo Guzmàn, the leading drug trafficker of all time, is still alive.

1947-

O. J. Simpson, after killing his ex-wife and her boyfriend, is still alive.

1961-

Joseph Kony, after displacing over 2 million people, abducting

60,000, including 30,000 children and forcing them to fight in his campaign of murder, rape, mutilation and sexual slavery, is still alive.

ENJOY THE JOURNEY

They say 'it's all about the journey, and not the destination'. I wholeheartedly agree with that.

The destination is the same for all of us. And it sucks. The only destination is death.

You can't escape it. I did a lot of research, but no one has ever beaten it.

You're going to die. But for now, you're alive and kicking! Hope you are enjoying yourself!

F?@K IT LIST II

'LIVING LIFE WITHOUT A GOAL,
IS LIKE LIVING LIFE IN A HOLE.'

So...how's it going? Feeling good? Still paying attention?

If you are following my instructions, and only reading one chapter at a time (I'm sure you tried to read a few at a time and realized that the potency of my thoughts was simply too overwhelming for full absorption and comprehension in a single day), then you will have taken a few days to get here. I just thought I'd check in and see how you're doing with your F?@k It List.

It's not a race or anything. But I bet you I'm winning.

Because if you really did write down your top five things for this year, my guess is that you felt pretty good that you gave it a few seconds of your precious time and thought about some happy moments that you could make happen for yourself. And then, in the very next minute, you said: 'Ah, screw it! The match is on.' Or, 'I have to finish that report.' Or, 'That girl I like will probably go to Royalty tonight and I can try to hit on her when she's smashed.'

I bet you didn't even consider doing the things on your list. You can't stop after you make the list, gandu (arsehole, just in case you didn't get it). Reading the list when it falls out of your diary, when you finally open it again after a few years, is not going to make you happy. Matter of fact, it will make you feel miserable that you still haven't done the things on the list. Big fail.

For best results, you actually have to do the things on your list. Ask me about my list. Come on, ask me.

Okay, so, here goes:

Shailendra Singh's F?@k It List

1. ~~Write the book that's been on my mind for so long.~~ (F?@k yeah!)
2. ~~Play a few good cricket matches with the Free Foresters, England.~~ (Killed it—man of the match!)
3. ~~Attempt the first twelve positions in the *Kama Sutra*.~~
4. ~~Get a trainer and a kick-ass training schedule.~~ (Wanna feel my pecs?)
5. ~~Give up sweets.~~ (I was raised by a sugar technologist's wife. This one was sooooo friggin' hard...)
6. Hike from Gangotri to Nanda Devi.

Five down, one more to go! For years, I've wanted to go to Gangotri and hike across the meadows and over the mountain passes to the glacier. The source of the Ganges. The mouth of the Mighty Mother.

Unfortunately, I've been too busy chasing my freaking tail around the boardroom for the last few years, and the glaciers have been melting at an alarming rate. If I wait any longer, they might just be gone altogether. And then we'll all be fighting for clean drinking water and everybody's F?@k It List will get f?@ked anyway.

Anyhoo... Here's the trick to fulfilling your F?@k It List:

Your generation has subscribed to and consumed the Nike mentality like it's going out of style—'Just do it'. The truth of the matter is that it *is* going out of style. It's not cool to say 'Just do it' any more.

You know what's f?@king cool? It's goddamn cool to say, 'Just DONE it.'

Don't tell me what you're *going to do*. You keep that nicely written down on your list, and tucked under the porn mags in your dresser drawer, tacked and gathering dust on the bulletin board in your office or locked in your memory box.

When you meet me next, and offer to buy me a vodka and lime, and I ask you—'What the hell has been going on, brother?', you should be able to look me in the eye and say, 'You know what's been going on, dude? I'll tell you what's going on. I finally got over my fear of heights.'

'Oh, shit, I remember! You wouldn't even go on the slide in preschool!'

'Yeah, man, well, I sucked it up, decided that it was time to confront it and I went skydiving.'

'Whoa! No f?@king way! Did you shit your pants?'

'Funny you should ask that. I did actually. The moment that I realized my chute wasn't opening.'

'What?!'

'Yeah, man, my main chute released, but it was all tangled and never fully opened. I cut the main and pulled my reserve chute. That didn't open either. I knew it was the end for me. It was my worst fear coming true. My worst nightmare. I had that *exact* dream from the time I was a little boy.'

Dumbstruck silence.

'F?@k knows who was watching out for me that day, but I landed in a swamp. I must have hit the swamp just right. Obviously I lived, but I broke my back. Took me months to get back on my feet again.'

It's supposed to be 'Just done it'. Not 'done in'!

F?@K KNOWS WHY THE WORD 'SUICIDE' IS CALLED 'KHUD KHUSHI' IN HINDI

'I'M UNHAPPY BECAUSE I DON'T WANT TO BE HAPPY.'

In English, the definition of 'suicide' is: 'self-imposed death'. But in Hindi, the equivalent of suicide is 'khud khushi', which literally translates to 'self-happiness'.

Let that sink in. It's a deep thought.

I feel that contained within the Hindi meaning of the word is a complete philosophy of life. Basically, if you are not living life in complete and utter happiness, then you're just asking for death.

To further simplify this, I would suggest that it means that you are born to be happy, you should live your life happily, and if you are somehow not able to do that, then it's as good as killing yourself slowly, day by day.

There's a certain sense of entitlement within the Hindi word; a selfishness to be able to determine the course of your own life, or lack thereof. Osho stresses this a lot, that it is good to be selfish. To make yourself happy first, and then look to make others happy. Another group of wise individuals also preach this on a daily basis: air hostesses.

I never listen to the safety instructions on a flight. I've heard the spiel a trillion times. By the time they hold up and start buckling the fake seatbelt, I've usually got my earbuds jammed deep into my ears, and am already flying away with Norah Jones or Infected Mushroom.

But the most memorable part of the safety speech, the part that always jumps out when you do listen, is when you are advised, in case of loss of air pressure in the cabin, that 'if you are travelling with a child, attend to yourself first, then to the child or anyone else in need of assistance'.

Quite the opposite of what we have been taught throughout life. The children always come first. But the pretty, well-groomed air hostess is right, if you do not have oxygen in your lungs, and you are not in good shape, how the f?@k will you take care of a child or anyone else? It just makes sense. You have to look out for yourself first, before you can tackle other things.

Once your umbilical cord is cut, and you are an independent little brat, with an independent soul and an independent heart, it's your responsibility to take care of your own happiness. Once they don't have to blow your nose and wipe your ass for you any more, no one, not even your parents, is going to take on the job of your happiness. They've got their own happiness, or sadness, to think about.

So it's all up to you. You are the one who can make or break your enjoyment of this life. And, if you can't find happiness in this life, well then, what's the friggin' point? Who's to say that death isn't a whole hell of a lot better?

Again, again. Don't get me wrong. You're always doing this! You're always misunderstanding me…

I'm not saying that if you're having a bad day, that you should just go slit your wrists. That because you are having a bad streak in business and in relationships and at the card tables, you should just end it once and for all. I'm not saying that death is a better option.

I'm just saying that, in understanding the meaning of 'khud khushi', we realize that our happiness is in our control. Our day-to-day happiness and our most ultimate happiness.

I'll tell you a story to explain...

I have a problem. I am constantly happy. I am always smiling. And smiling full-on. You can see it in all the photos. My big, toothy, open-mouthed smile. You rarely catch me without it. I'm a friggin' happy guy.

Now that's not a problem for me, and it didn't seem to bother anyone when I was younger. As I grew up, though, I started getting comments from the people around me, starting with my mother. 'Beta, what's wrong with you? You can't be so happy all the time. Are you covering up for something? What's wrong?'

'Uh, I'm fine, ma.'

'Well then, why can't you pose for photographs like a normal person?'

And then, from a client, 'Dude, you are, like, so happy all the time! What are you on?'

'On? As in...?'

'What drugs are you taking, man?'

'No way! I don't take drugs. I'm high on life, bro!'

And then from a (so-called) friend, 'Shailu, you're always so happy. You're never down. Is that really possible? You know, you can tell me anything. You can tell me your troubles and your worries. You don't have to hide all the bad stuff. Don't you trust me?'

It came to a point when, every time I attended a party, people would immediately ask me, 'Yo, Shail. You're looking happy! What happened? You just made some big money? You won an award?

You f?@ked up a competitor? Why the big smile?'

After a few times of telling people that I was simply happy, that my heart was beating and my lungs were doing their bit, I gave up. That didn't seem to be a believable answer.

Being sad, being disturbed, being stressed and worried all the time, seems to be the 'in' thing. Being grumpy is cool. My guesstimate is that, in this age of economics instead of emotion, stressing yourself out trying to earn and falling into depression when the stock market crashes is a badge of honour. It means you're in the game.

If someone else is ridiculously happy, it means they're playing a different game, and that's just not fair. Or cool. And about five years ago, I started to play their game. I fell into the trap. Things weren't really going my way, on a number of fronts, and I took membership in the 'My Life is F?@ked, I'm Really Sad Club'.

I played the role well. I stopped smiling. I stopped shaving. I started complaining and whining that the world was out to get me. I blamed anything and everything for my unhappiness, except for myself.

And then, I woke up one morning, and I said, what's the point of living all of this; if I am not happy, what's the friggin' point? And I decided to kill that miserable Shailendra Singh. I used something sharper than a razor and more powerful than a gun. I used my heart.

My heart was beating heavy and hollow those days. I listened to it, I told it I understood its pain, I hadn't been focusing on the right things lately. I apologized and I asked it if, together, we couldn't do something about that? I promised to shift my focus back to appreciating the things that I had—a devoted wife, an adorable son, two and a half brilliant friends, a hard-earned career, true wealth and health—and to stop focusing on the things that

I didn't have. And I asked my heart, in return, to beat a little bit lighter and with a lot more spirit each and every day.

I committed khud khushi. I took responsibility for my happiness and now I'm back!

I am living in the skin that I was born to live in. I am f?@king happy. I f?@king love this life.

All you f?@kers can go be sad. I don't care what the hell you do. Just don't go blaming anyone or anything else for your miserable existence. You have only yourself to blame. And only you have the power of your own khud khushi.

CTRL + ALT + DELETE

'YOU HAVE THE POWER TO DESTROY WHAT YOU
HAVE BUILT, AND BUILD AGAIN.'

Sit back for a moment, put the book down, and take a good long look at your life. Are you healthy and breathing? Do you have the basic necessities you need to thrive—food, clothing, shelter, mobility? Are you comfortable?

If the answer to all those questions is 'yes', then here's the kicker: Are you genuinely happy?

If you have everything you need—good health, a good education, a great job, a decent car, a nice girl/boyfriend—and you find that you're still not truly happy, then either you're just a really miserable person, or you've taken a wrong turn on your journey. Maybe you really wanted to be a fashion designer, but, at your dad's insistence, you studied to be an engineer. Just like your dad, and his dad, and his dad before that. Maybe you're a free soul who needs trees and flowers and butterflies to walk amongst, but you live in the city because that's where all the good jobs are. Maybe your boyfriend is really not 'the one'.

If you are not happy, even if you have it all, then f?@k, man, it's time to start over. It's time to reboot.

I've seen a lot of people like this throughout my life. They have everything that they could possibly want and yet they aren't happy. Most of them have continued to do the same thing day after day, hoping for different results ('Insanity', Einstein tells us). Fifteen years later, they are still unhappy. A few of them, though, have said, 'enough is enough', and jumped out of their skin and started doing things differently. These people have made magic happen in their lives.

This also happens when people have an accident or 'incident'. They get shaken up. They get thrown out of their routine, make big changes, and go back to the things that are important. So, if you are unhappy, even though you have every reason to be happy, you can either shake yourself out of your skin, or wait until a car crash or a severe illness changes your perspective on life. Either way, I highly recommend you try it.

It's a scary thought to start again. You've travelled so far. You are comfortable with where you are in life, secure. You have habits and routines that you follow. You know, for the most part, what you can expect out of your day. The thought of leaving that comfort zone and restarting, embarking upon a new journey full of unknowns and imponderables, can send a shiver down your spine.

But it's not as scary as you think. Humans are very versatile and adaptable creatures. We have the potential to live many different lives in one life, but we rarely take the risk. I'm not a doctor. I'm not a guru or a guide who can convince you to do it or show you how. I can just tell you what I did.

At forty-five years, I had done it all. I had been there and done that. I had everything that I could possibly want in the world. But I was seriously confused as to where I was supposed to go next. I knew that I didn't want to keep living in the same skin, I was done with that one. I was ready for a new Shailendra Singh. But which skin was I to put on? Who was I to be?

I decided to start at the beginning. I decided I needed to be born again. To reboot. So, I went back to the place of my birth. It was a long road trip, but once I reached the town of my birth, I drove straight to the hospital that I was born in. I parked my car, walked into the reception and took a good look around. I wanted to feel the hospital where I first breathed life. I wanted to ask if any of the nurses who had helped deliver me were still around. But once I smelled the hospital and saw the IV units being wheeled down the hall, I turned around and ran back to my car. I f?@king hate hospitals.

I drove to my first school. I could barely remember walking through those front doors every day, but I tried to imagine what I used to think, what I used to feel back then. Then I went to my second school. I asked the secretary for the teacher roster and actually recognized two names on the list. I was directed to the office of my old reading and writing teacher. Amazingly, she remembered me. 'Of course I remember you,' she said. 'Your writing was atrocious. Used to take me an hour to read your papers. Nowadays, we have special classes for children with dyslexia.'

I went back to my college and had the cutting chai and vada pao that I used to survive on in those days. As I sat and ate in the courtyard, I tried to remember my state of mind, my thought processes, my dreams and desires, when I went to college there. How had they changed since then? What had I compromised on? What had I forgotten?

Soon after, no lie, I had to travel to the UK on work. I took a quick flight to Scotland, to a place called Dundee, where I had played my first amateur county game. I sat on the bench at my field and relived that day, twenty-nine years ago, when I bowled my first ball in England. That was the most vivid memory of the rebooting, so far. I tracked down my cricket coach—it's a small town—and knocked on his door.

'Well, I'll be,' he said, and invited me in for tea. We reminisced about the good old days and talked about where life had taken us.

When I flew back to Mumbai, I shut my eyes and relived the flight that I had taken, so many years ago. The one that left the cricket fields behind and brought me back to the city to 'get a real job'. I remembered how it felt like the end of a chapter that I didn't want to close, and I remembered why I had needed to do it.

Long story short, I had reconnected with my beginning. I walked through the places and met some of the people who had laid the foundation of my beliefs and my emotions. In the process of learning who I was, I realized a lot about who I am. And about why I didn't become someone else.

I found myself in shunya space. Zero space. A kind of no-man's land that would leave some people terrified. Adrift. But I was liberated. By reliving my past, I had left it behind. A much-needed ending and a bright new beginning. I was fresh. New. Able to start again. Rebooted, without the errors.

I knew which skin it was now time to live in.

'DON'T LET THE DOOR HIT YOU ON YOUR WAY OUT'

'EVERY TIME YOU SAY "YES" TO SOMETHING USELESS,
YOU SAY "NO" TO SOMETHING THAT IS BLOODY IMPORTANT.'

If you want to reboot your life, if you want to wear a different skin for a while, there are many ways to do it. I recommend the 'return to your birthplace' method, but you could probably do it through a simple change of geography—moving to a new country and assuming a new identity—or possibly through hypnosis. You could do mind exercises—visualizing a number of doors in front of you, and choosing which door you want to walk through.

However you do it, there is one absolutely crucial element that you have to keep in mind. And if you don't do it, you won't succeed.

Human beings are creatures of habit and security. We are fickle. We like to hedge our bets and keep escape routes ready in case something goes wrong. If we want to open a new door, we want to keep the old door open, just in case.

'Why don't I just open this door, stick my head inside and have a look-see? But I'll leave this door open too, just in case. I'll see if things are looking better over there than over here, and then make up my mind!'

You cannot do that. It will not work. If you keep two doors open, you will have one foot inside one room and the other foot inside another room. You will remain stuck in the middle, never giving either your 100 per cent, and are sure to find only frustration.

I kept four doors open for four years. I stayed in the room I was living in—working my ass off from morning till night to run my company—but kept opening the doors to three other rooms that I really wanted to visit. The first door was a social initiative: I wanted to make a cross-country bicycle trip to raise awareness for the cause of HIV/AIDS. The second door was a travel adventure: I wanted to climb Kilimanjaro. And the third door was a creative challenge: I wanted to write a book. I wanted to go through those doors so bad, but I just couldn't shut the first one. I left them all open and caught a terrible draft. Instead of finding my happiness, I had a terrible cold for four straight years.

I was too busy in the boardroom to plan the trip to Kilimanjaro. Now the ice caps are melting at an alarming rate, and I might never get to see them. I was too busy selling myself to clients, even after years of getting 99 per cent strike rates for them, to plan the cross-country bicycle trip for AIDS awareness. I read in the paper yesterday that three people, all above fifty years, have just driven from London to Bombay, crossing twelve countries in twenty-three days, to create awareness for blood cancer. They did it. I didn't.

If I had just shut that first door, I could have opened so many other doors in those four years. They could have been bad rooms, they could have been fantastic rooms. F?@k knows!

But I'm happy to report, that after four years, I finally did it. I finally followed my own advice of ditching the 'Just do it!' to 'Just done it!' I finally shut that old door and opened a new one, my first: the creative challenge. You can make your own decision as to whether it was worth it to give this book to the world, but I think it was a damn good choice.

SIGNS

'PROBLEMS ARE NOTHING BUT SOLUTIONS,
IN A MASK OF FEAR AND ANXIETY.'

We are all born with infinite possibilities. We can become the prime minister of the country, the president or the Pope. So why do we become carpenters, accountants, business people or janitors?

Now don't get all dramatic on me. All professions are good and respected and necessary. The Pope shouldn't get more respect than a janitor, since, at the end of the day, they are both human beings. But, let's face it, would you rather scrub shit stains off the toilet, or dictate the course of millions of people's lives around the world?

I believe that we are all born equal and will die equal. So then what is it that determines the direction of our lives? What determines our ambition, our skills and our commitment? Is it destiny or fate? Or can we get a bit scientific and blame it on our DNA?

If it is all about the DNA, then you're f?@king screwed. You can give up trying to fix your life, because you're already jacked. You can't change what you've been given. If your mom and dad together made an ambitionless ass, then what can you do? But you *can* help out with the generation that follows yours. You can find the most talented possible partner you can successfully seduce and mate with them. Maybe a mathematician, scientist or astronaut, get the sperm or egg of that genius, and 'whoops', you can have a daughter or son with exactly the talents you wanted.

If it were that simple, sperm/eggs would have become more precious then uranium. We would not have to fear the threat of nuclear bombs, we would have to worry about sperm/egg bombs.

But it's not true, is it? Just look at me. My dad was a tall, handsome, hard-working, honest sugar technologist. I, his third son, am only an average-looking, gorilla shaped, bullshitting marketing professional. Where did the DNA go wrong?

So, if it's not all in the DNA, then it must be the decisions that you make and the actions that you take that determine the course of your life. It's hard to think that's the prime driver. Janitors and street cleaners work harder than most corporate employees that I know, but they don't seem to reap equal rewards for their efforts. And, you have to admit, we always face strange circumstances in our lives. Moments that make you feel like, 'Seriously, this is happening this way. Go figure!'

I deeply believe that, starting at a very early age in our lives, we receive signs. We get callings. You may call it coincidence, you may call it fate. I don't know what to call it. It's very hard to explain. It's hard for me to wrap my mind around it.

But why do you meet just those thousand people on the planet, and not the other thousand that you could have possibly met? Why do you end up going to England, and not to Ireland? Why do you manage to somehow catch the double-decker bus, and not the single decker? Why did you kiss Betty when you had your eyes on Veronica?

In life, you get messages from up there, out there. You get signs to tell you there are doors and options open to you. But then, the call is yours. If you notice, you usually have two options in all circumstances, and you generally tend to pick the one that you are most comfortable with. Hardly anyone takes the path that is challenging and unknown. But the option is there.

I loved the movie—yup, you guessed it—*Sliding Doors*, starring Gwyneth Paltrow. What a concept. The premise of the movie poses so many questions that are relevant to choosing that other path. What happens if you don't catch that train? What happens if you come home just a few minutes earlier? Such a small, seemingly insignificant moment could be life altering, without you even knowing it. My God!

In the movie, Gwyneth's life takes two drastically different routes. In the first scenario, she boards the early train and catches her boyfriend cheating on her, she dumps him and then meets the true love of her life, but then she gets hit by a car and ends up in the hospital in a coma. In the second scenario, circumstances shift ever so slightly—she misses her train, gets mugged, comes home late, doesn't catch her man cheating and sticks with the deadbeat until his other girlfriend shows up and tells her she's pregnant with his child. She can't see through her tears as she runs out of the apartment, when she falls down the stairs and ends up in the hospital in a coma. You are hoping for her to come out of her coma in the first scenario, but she doesn't. She dies in that one. She wakes up in the second scenario, but tells her boyfriend to hit the road. In the elevator, on her way out of the hospital, however, she meets a stranger who is actually her true love from the first scenario. They were meant to be together. She just took a different path to get there.

So…basically, what the movie says is that we are slated and fated for certain things, but the path to get there is determined by the decisions that we take. At least I think that's what it means.

◆

I'm writing this chapter sitting in front of Winchester Cathedral. I took a trip here just so I could write a few chapters. I came to Winchester four years ago to play a cricket match. I love Winchester. The very first cricket pitch in the country was built here by the same man who built Lord's. Yesterday, I played on the Winchester college ground, where Douglas Jardine played. These are just a few reasons that I love the place.

But four years ago, I had never heard of Winchester. I just came for the cricket. After my match, I returned to the Holiday Inn where I was staying and found a brochure about the Winchester Cathedral lying on my bedside table. A visit to the cathedral was highly recommended. I made it just in time for evening mass. I attended the first mass of my life in a cathedral ranked number one in Europe.

While I sat listening to the sermon, I felt the energy of my father. I could feel him close to me. I felt him rest his hand gently on my shoulder. I'm still not a fan of Christ, but now, I am a huge fan of the energy that I get in the cathedral in Winchester.

Years later, as I sat in Mumbai, the city that had so far determined my career, my fate, my destiny, I felt like I was being destroyed piece by piece, with every breath I took. I wasn't inspired to write. I needed an escape. I wanted to get lost to find myself. It was then that I remembered Winchester. And as I write this chapter, sitting just outside the cathedral, with the light sparkling off the stained glass windows, I am feeling...open. I am feeling receptive. I feel like I am seeing these little signs to guide my way, which were probably there before, but which I never noticed. And I think they are leading me to amazing places!

While I was walking to a cute little corner bistro that I remembered from my first trip, I took a wrong turn. I found a fantastic little two-screen movie theatre. They were playing *The*

Avengers and *Salmon Fishing in the Yemen*. I would have seen either, but, when I went to the counter, I ended up buying tickets to the Bob Marley documentary that they were to screen in five days. I hate documentaries, I never plan so far ahead and I had no idea if I would even be in Winchester in five days time, but I bought the tickets.

I didn't know what a true rock star Bob Marley was. I didn't know about his political voice. I didn't know he died of cancer. F?@k man, at the age of thirty-six. The movie moved me. Bob Marley was a man driven by passion. However long or short, blessed or troubled life is, a life without passion is not a life worth living.

I don't know how I found that cinema that day. I don't know why I had to go all the way to Winchester to sit close to my father. I don't know how it's all happening, but I sure am having fun experiencing it.

WHAT GOES IN,
MUST COME OUT—BODY

'IN INDIA, WE ARE BLESSED WITH CUISINE
THAT YOU EAT ONCE, BUT ENJOY TWICE.'

You've heard the old saying: 'You are what you eat'? Figuratively speaking, it's a nice thought. Literally speaking, however, it's off the mark. If you eat lots of carrots, you aren't going to turn orange and start growing leafy greens out of the top of your head. If you eat lots of chicken, you aren't going to start laying eggs (although you may start developing bigger boobs from all the growth hormones that they force-feed those suckers).

Much more accurate is the saying: 'What goes in, must come out'. If you eat lots of fatty red meat, your shit is going to float. If you eat lots of corn, your crap will have a nice yellow, mosaic styling in the morning. Not enough fibre? It might not come out at all.

When I was young, I was a vacuum cleaner. I would eat anything, from anywhere, at any time. One day, after an early evening sugar fix at Shamiana Coffee Shop, an old woman came over to me and said, 'Beta, I've been watching you. Do you realize what you have just eaten?'

'Uh, yes ma'am. I've had a tub of chikoo ice cream, two Mars bars and three bags of M&Ms.'

'Why aren't you eating a proper dinner, beta? You can't have only sweets for dinner.'

'No, ma'am. You're right ma'am. Dinner is at home, in one hour.'

She paused, a bit in shock, and then slowly, sat down across from me. 'You should be in the *Guinness Book of World Records* right now, for not throwing up. But, young man, you can't continue to eat like this. I want you to do me a favour. Will you be a good boy and do it for me? Tomorrow, during the day, from morning until night, whatever you put into your mouth, anything at all that you eat, I want you to put the same thing, in the same amount, into a glass jar. In your case, a very big glass jar. At the end of the day, before sleeping, take a good, long look at the contents of that jar. Realize that everything squishing together in that jar, rotting away in the Mumbai heat, is exactly what is filling your stomach as you lay down to sleep.'

That sounded totally gross. But at that age, gross is awesome, so I did it. I told Mom it was a science experiment for school, so she agreed to make double portions.

Breakfast was Coco Pops with milk and jaggery, two toasts, an omelette, a banana and a Mars bar. Lunch was palak paneer, dal, chicken kadai, achar, three rotis, rice, gulab jamun and a Mars bar. Teatime was two Cokes instead of tea, four Bourbon biscuits, a Mango Duet and two bags of M&Ms. Dinner was chicken makhni, aloo gobi, raita, three rotis, rice and a giant frickin' bowl of ghee-licious halwa.

At the end of that day, looking into that jar at the partially decomposing food mixture—some bits starting to break down in the Coke, most still as solid as I had dropped them in, the milk curdling, the rice slipping into all the empty spaces with the help of the separating raita—I was way more grossed out than I thought I would be.

It was a nasty combination of colours and smells. And there was so much of it! How could I possibly expect my body to digest it all, circulate the good stuff, and produce nice, healthy sausages to feed the pot?

I checked in the morning. My sausages were definitely not healthy.

If you put crap into your body, crap is going to come out. If you put healthy, nutritious food into your body, then…well… okay, crap is still going to come out. But it will be much healthier crap. Healthier, as in…well…see… Apparently, it's supposed to be brown (because of the bile in the stomach), 'comfortable to pass' and it is supposed to smell (because of the bacteria in the gut).

You get what I'm saying right? You know when it's right. (And you know you wonder when you see all those ridiculously fat children stuffing their face with french fries at McDonald's. All that grease and fatty food, their shit must float right out of the bathroom like helium balloons.)

As you get older, you start to really feel the effects of each and every item that you put into your system. A little too much spice, a little too much oil, and you notice the changes almost instantly. A little cramp, a little bloating, some gas bubbles. You may think it's fine right now, lying in your dorm room, reading this book and farting away, not caring if your stupid roommate has to smell your semi-digested pizza and chicken wings.

But, when you start to work and share an AC-only, windowless office with someone, then it's kind of nice to be 'regular'. When you're in a board meeting, trying to close a big sponsorship deal, you don't want to have to go running to the loo to get rid of that pani puri and bhel puri that you gobbled up on the street for breakfast. Elevator rides to the thirty-first floor, carpools, squash games with a client—all can be ruined by a nasty stinker that just *has* to come out.

It is most important to exercise regularly when you start to date. When you have someone lying next to you, whom you wish to leave a decent impression on, well then, those stomach rumblings become quite embarrassing.

Yeah, I think you get the point. What goes in, must come out. Pay attention to what you put in, because, when there's a pretty girl lying naked on your bed, spooning you from the back, you don't want strange things to come out.

WHAT GOES IN,
MUST COME OUT—MIND

'THE MIND IS A DEVIL THAT CONSUMES AND KEEPS.'

It's the same with your mind. What you put in, must come out.
If you watch the news before sleeping, you will surely have
nightmares. You'll probably be kidnapped by Somalian pirates,
shot in the head by Syrian troops, drowned when your overloaded
rescue boat capsizes, all in one night. Brutal.

If you watch Hindi soaps in the afternoon, you will start
to suspect that your stepdaughter is trying to poison you, your
two eldest sons are fighting over the recently widowed (under
mysterious circumstances) woman next door, and your husband
is under the spell of a vindictive witch. Playing violent video
games surely does make kids numb to violence, although I'm
not sure it makes them violent as well. If all your friends are
chain-smoking depressives, complaining every day that they 'just
can't cut a break', then it's going to be really hard for you to
keep smiling every day.

Everything that you listen to, all the rubbish that people say—
the gossip and the nonsense that people feed you—will eventually
get processed. It will absorb into your grey matter in ways that
you won't even realize. And it will have to come out.

The complaints, the nagging, the sadness, the aggression, the
general bad energies and bad attitudes of other people will soak

into your system. You might not feel the effects at that moment, you may be able to keep smiling and stay optimistic, but it will gradually affect your heartbeat. Slowly but surely, your attitude will change for the worse, your optimism will wane and you'll start complaining about everyone and everything. If negativity is all you see and hear all day, you will eventually start to fit the mold.

It's important to surround yourself with good people, good thoughts and good energy. If happy people surround you, it is so much easier for you to stay happy.

A simple thought, but easier said than done. You can't choose your family. That's pretty much decided before you're born, and they might be the most miserable people you have ever met. You can choose your friends, but everyone starts off with their best impression and with their game face on, and it might take you a while to realize that they are actually really terrible people. You compromise all the time on making acquaintances for the sake of business. In fact, the most aggressive, irritating people usually make the best business people. It's the nature of the beast.

So basically, you're f?@ked, because it's really, really hard to find happy people who only throw good energy and happy thoughts your way.

But don't despair! There is a solution!

There is a way to protect yourself from absorbing the unnecessary and unwanted energies in your daily life!

Brought to you by the creator of the patented 'Chi F?@k Breathing Method', this art is a breakthrough in the mastery of input assimilation and mindful decision-making!

Based on the art of Tai Chi, but adapted for use in the modern age!

A strategy for filtering the bullshit that comes your way!

It can be yours today, and today only, as a bonus for all the hard work you have put in towards learning and practicing the 'Chi F?@k Breathing Method'!

If you are ready to change your life and make your heart beat happier and healthier, then just turn the page!

CHI F?@K PO

"'NO" IS THE NEW "YES".'

Introducing the art of physically expressing your power of choice—Chi F?@k Po! (Po is short for 'positions', 'poses', 'postures' and/or 'possibilities'.)

Chi F?@k Po is a mental exercise to consciously filter the input being thrown your way, all day, every day. It trains you to truly exercise your freedom to choose, by deciding which information you absorb and integrate.

Since we have realized that our mind is easily deceived and deceitful, I have enhanced the exercise with a strong physical component, which brings about incredible focus in order to avoid deception.

It is loosely based on the skills and techniques of Tai Chi. If you don't know jack about Tai Chi, it doesn't matter, because it's nothing at all like Tai Chi, really.

Chi F?@k Po is pretty simple. Just four easy steps:

B. Block.
C. Choose.
D. Divert.
E. Embrace.

Scenario:

It's 4 p.m. in the evening, you are sitting on the terrace having tea with your mother and watching the sun set slowly in the sky. After concluding a brief discussion over why you didn't make it home until 6 a.m. in the morning ('I fell asleep playing a rousing game of Monopoly at a friend's house. Would I lie to you, mom?'), your mother says, 'You know, beta, I don't understand why you want to write a book. You're not an author. No one's going to publish it. You're just going to end up spending all your own money to make it and get it printed. Why don't you focus on something more reasonable, no?'

Step 1: **Block**

The first reaction is always to block whatever is coming at you. Whether it's stress from a parent to get married quickly because you are 'losing your glow', cubicle drama from a gossipmonger workmate, criticism for your constant use of the word 'f?@k'— let's just call them all 'provocatives'. Whatever is coming at you, hoping to provoke you, block it.

Do not let it hit you. Physically, you have to step one foot forward, like when lunging, but only a pace apart. This is to improve your balance and increase your strength against the onslaught. At the same time, put your arms straight out in front of you, kind of like if you were to make a cross with your fingers to ward off the devil, but with your palms open and facing the front. This is your defence shield, to stop the provocative from reaching you. I call it the 'No Po'.

You are blocking physically, to give yourself a pause, mentally. You need time to consider what's going on. You need time to make a choice. If you don't block it, and it hits you, you're screwed.

Good, bad or ugly, if the provocative is not originating from within you, then it will always create conflict when it's absorbed. You may forget about it an hour later, but, in that moment when it hits you, it will leave a mark. Your mind hears it, your body feels it, and your heart will start to beat just a little bit differently.

When someone, especially someone that you love, tells you that 'you are going to fail if you try something new', block it. Don't let it in. Keep it at arm's length. Don't react. Wait.

For the sake of self-preservation, your natural instinct should be to block everything.

Step 2: **Choose**

So now, you are standing strong in the 'No Po', and blocking the provocative that's floating right there in front of you. The provocative is very mad. It's banging up against you, pushing, trying to get in. 'Hear me! React to me! Do this! Don't do this! Bang! Bang! Bang!'

Now you have to decide what you are going to do with it. You need a moment—just a moment—to decide whether you like it, don't like it, agree, don't agree, believe or don't believe in its message. And you have to decide in a split second. Your first instinct, your first gut reaction, is always right. The longer you think about it, the more confused you will get.

Ask yourself, 'Is this good for me?' and listen to what your gut has to say.

Step 3: **Divert** or **Embrace**

If the answer to the question, 'Is this good for me?' is 'No', or if you are unsure, have a 'funny feeling', or any sort of doubt at all, then you have to push the provocative aside. You have to reject it. With your palms facing outward, you simply guide the unwanted provocative around the left side or the right side of your body. Just let it slip past you and fall somewhere, abandoned, in the dirt behind you.

This is called, 'Let-go Po'.

If the answer to the question 'Is this good for me?' is a strong and clear 'Yes' from your gut, then you need to take the provocative in, and take it in quickly. You have to embrace it while it is still pure. You can't let the mind get a hold of it, or it will prostitute it with multiple thoughts.

If your girlfriend tells you that she loves you for the first time, then your heart and your gut will rejoice, 'Yay! Yay! Yay!' But within a fraction of a second, your mind will start to shout, 'Yeah, sure! It feels that way now, buddy, but she's probably just seducing you so that she can push you down the stairs, and take your money, the penthouse and the Porsche.'

Keep it pure. Take it in quickly. Use your hands to scoop the provocative towards you, molding it into a condensed ball. Bring it close to your body, and press it into your gut. Absorb it straight into your core. Hide it deep and securely, so that your mind can't reach it. It is now a part of you. It is you.

This is called, 'My Po'.

That is Chi F?@k! It's as simple as that.

You can't be shy with the physical actions, with the blocking and the casting away of the provocatives. Your mind will not be strong enough to carry out the process without the discipline of your body. (At least not at first, until you make the whole process a good habit.) Other people may find it weird, but once they realize that you are actually filtering all the bullshit that they are throwing at you, they'll be like, 'WTF? She's not listening to me! I'm not affecting him! I'm not getting the reaction I hoped for.' And then they'll go trouble someone else with their rubbish. Success!

Think of Chi F?@k Po like it's a super power. Your invisible force field, blocking all that is negative and unhealthy, impenetrable by anything that is not good and pure. And even then, it works based on your choosing to let the provocative into your body, mind and soul. Only if you choose to make it a part of you.

If you only take in the good stuff, only good stuff will come out. Just like with your bowel movements. You will be a better, more consistent person. A more likeable person. And when more people like you, you'll feel loved and will be happy, which will attract even more happy people and things into your life. See how that works?

You have the power to choose happiness. So throw your hands up in the air, block your boyfriend, block your boss, block your accountant, block your teacher, block your priest, block them right in the face. As you take their provocative, neutralize it and toss it aside. Make sure to throw in a loud 'CHI F?@K!' for good measure.

STOP THINKING, START DOING

'DREAM AND DO IT.
OR KEEP WAITING TO DREAM, AND DIE.'

How does life work? Or rather, how do you work, in this life?

You have a thought.

You believe in your thought.

You execute that thought.

You feel happy that you:

- thought,
- believed in,
- and executed that thought.

It's that simple.

I can always count on my wife to tell me things straight. She's a big fan of mine, and listens to all my gyaan ('knowledge', sarcastically) with a patient ear and an open mind. But when she does have something to say, it is usually spot on.

'Babs (that's me),' she said to me one day. 'You say a lot of great things. You give a lot of great advice. You make a lot of sense. Just do me one favour, Babs… Start *doing* the things you say.'

Oof. Shit. Of course she was right. I talk a lot. I feel like I know a lot of things and I tell a lot of people 'how it goes'. But how much of it do I take action on?

I decided to try it, the next chance I got. When we went

out for dinner that night, I tipped my steward at the start of the meal. It was something that I had talked about doing for many years, impressing people with my opinion and logic, but had never actually done.

So I finally just did it. Instead of putting value to the service he would have given us that night, I encouraged better service by giving him value. I was clear in my intention to have a good time that night: I had taken the effort to pick that particular restaurant, selected the companions that would indulge and entertain me, and even requested the table in the corner, by the window. I had choreographed everything, so why not choreograph excellent service?

It worked. The steward was damn motivated to perform his duty to the best of his ability. He wasn't doing tricks, performing for a handout at the end of the meal. I had appreciated his job at the start, and given him value for being able to make or break my night. For me, that night, he took extra pride in doing his best.

Sure, he must have also thought that, if I could afford to tip him up front, I might tip him more at the end, too. That's a fair assumption, and may have served to inspire even more diligent service.

Seems like common sense, no? But yet, no one I know does it. Now I do it every time I go out. I choreograph my service, and my enjoyment.

That was a simple story, not very philosophical. But the majority of our thoughts are simple. We have a zillion of them in a day. There are so many things that we think of doing. Most of them we don't do. But when we do them, when we make a simple change, or fix a simple problem, the impact can be huge. And, if we did just ten of the zillion that we think in a day... whoa! What an impact that could make.

At the root of everything, we each know what we really   ...,
how we want it, and when we want it. We have the power to
imagine everything just as we would like it to be, but we don't
believe in ourselves enough to actually make it happen.

The best way to gain confidence about our ideas is to try
them out—put your thoughts to the test, and see what happens.
The more you put your ideas to the test and see them succeed,
the more trust you will have in yourself to choreograph your
success. Even if they fail, you will realize that failing isn't so bad,
and you will find the strength to try again.

Every day I wake up knowing exactly what I want, and I go
out and get it. Ninety-nine times out of hundred, I choreograph
my success. It's not that hard, actually. It's simply the difference
between thinking 'Just do it' and saying 'Just done it!'

You are capable of navigating this life. You just have to believe
that you are. Follow through on your thoughts and ideas. And
you'll see what magic you can make happen.

YOU DON'T *HAVE* TO DO ANYTHING

'YOU DO REALIZE THAT YOU ARE 100 PER CENT ACCOUNTABLE
FOR EVERY DECISION THAT YOU MAKE. NO ONE ELSE IS TO
BLAME. YOU ARE A RATIONAL BEING, AND ONLY YOU WILL BE
HELD ACCOUNTABLE.'

As you politely excuse yourself from the dinner table, is it really appropriate to say 'I *have* to take a shit'? Unless you drank some really rank, smashed-fly-infused sugar-cane juice from the side of the road earlier (he doesn't have running water, so how do you think he washes those glasses?), then your shit is not holding a gun to your anus and saying: 'Let me out now, motherf?@ker!'

Isn't it more appropriate to inform your dinner guests like so: 'I want to take a shit'?

In most cases, the shit is just hanging around, saying, 'Hey dude! I'm here. You can let me loose whenever you feel like it. Oh, you're ready now? Great. Okay. Here we go! Wheee! That was fun. Now flush me! Flush me! Wheee! Byeee!'

The secret to living life at a flow and, at the risk of sounding poetic, constantly having a glow, is to realize that you don't *have* to do anything. You do things because you *want* to do them.

This sounds very uncomplicated and simple, but surprisingly— if you notice—from the time we wake up until the time that we go to sleep, the words that we use to express ourselves tell a different story: 'I have to go to work. I have to go for a meeting. I have to do my homework. I have to take a flight. I have to brush my teeth. I have to marry my girlfriend. I have to finish my boss's presentation.'

The Oxford Dictionary meaning of the phrase 'have to' is to 'be obliged or find it necessary to do a specified thing'. Who are you obliged to? Who have you promised that every day you will wake up and go to work? If anyone, it's you. By desiring a paycheck so that you can buy trendier clothes, better cars and get hotter girlfriends, you are obliged to go to work. It's what *you* want. No one is holding a gun to your head. But by saying 'I have to' all day, that's what it sounds like. That perspective is sure to make anyone miserable.

The Oxford Dictionary meaning of the phrase 'want to' is to 'have a desire to possess or do (something); wish for'. Now doesn't that sound so much better?

By the choices you have made in the past, the decisions that you take in the present and the goals you have set for the future, you are determining what happens in your day. You don't 'have to' do any of it. You have chosen it to be this way. You might as well take responsibility for your actions and enjoy them, because ideally, all these actions are pushing you closer to your goals.

The process is simple. Replace the words 'have to' with the words 'want to'. Say: 'I want to go to work, it's going to be a beautiful day!' 'I want to brush my teeth so that I feel fresh!' 'I want to do my homework, so I can get a good job as an elevator repairman!' 'I want to finish my boss's presentation, so that he doesn't fire me.' 'I want to marry my girlfriend, so that her father will stop pointing a gun at my head!'

Just replacing 'have to' with 'want to' changes the entire essence of your actions, and the spirit in which you make it happen.

100 PER CENT

'FOCUS CAN MOVE MOUNTAINS.'

Do things with all your heart. Do them with as much intensity as you are capable of.

Anything done half-heartedly will never bring you joy. It will only bring misery, anxiety and tension. Whenever you do anything half-heartedly, you are dividing yourself into two parts. You are leaving room for your mind to pick a fight with your heart. There will be conflict within you. Your heart will run left and your mind will run right; in short, you will create hell for yourself.

F?@k knows why we live most of our life divided in our thoughts and actions. Why we choose to create a hell for ourselves. Whether it be relationships or work, how often do we fully commit to something? We always doubt, we always hesitate. We fear failure. We fear rejection. We fear the hard work and pain it may take to get what we want.

Fear holds us back from giving our 100 per cent. We keep aside that 20-30 per cent to plan an escape route, to prepare excuses, to be able to say, 'Well, I didn't really try my hardest, so...'

Fear comes only from the mind. The heart knows what it wants. When you listen only to the heart, you are automatically of one mind. If you follow your heart then you will give a 100 per cent. It doesn't matter what you are doing, as long as you do it with all your heart, it will bring you joy!

Who knows what is right and what is wrong in this life? Sometimes the right way looks damn wrong when you get to the end, and sometimes the wrong way ends up seeming very right to everyone else involved. F?@k only knows. So then, why not commit to every action you choose, without doubt and without fear of it being wrong?

Life can be difficult enough. Don't complicate it further by living in two minds about everything. One mind, led by one heart. One choice. One hundred per cent effort. One result: Joy.

F?@K KNOWS WHERE OUR VALUES ARE

'OUR CIVILIZATION HAS CREATED ENOUGH BOMBS TO DESTROY
THE WORLD SEVERAL TIMES OVER. SO NOW CAN WE PLEASE
FOCUS ON THE SERIOUS ISSUES...
GLOBAL WARMING, HUNGER, EDUCATION,
ENDANGERED SPECIES?'

We used to admire surgeons and scientists and inventors: brilliant minds that healed, discovered and created. Now we worship actors, sportsmen and socialites: good-looking people who entertain, perform and go to parties.

We used to respect and admire great thinkers: philosophers with original theories about the meaning of life, writers who could inspire us to look at the world from a different perspective, physicists who had a theory and an atom particle named after them. We admired politicians who captained our nations and upheld the ideals of its people.

Nowadays, our society worships packaged icons: billionaires who have to pay famous women to date them so that no one knows they are gay, Bollywood actors whose movies are flops but who are still on the A-list because of a notable surname, politicians who have longer police records than those locked up in Tihar Prison.

Don't get me wrong, there has always been great admiration

for actors, pretty women and the rich and, therefore, the famous. But, in the past, they had usually achieved quite a lot by the time they became icons. Madhuri Dixit surely earned her place as India's leading lady after her performance in *Tezaab*. Meena Kumari and Madhubala gave some spectacular performances in some of the biggest classic movies of all time. Satyajit Ray made amazing cinema. These individuals became icons because they were creating brilliant content.

When you consider today's celebrities—the pop-culture heroes—what have most of them achieved besides being well-photographed socialites? What are they contributing to the country, or to culture? What legacy will they leave behind?

Not too long ago, we valued content. In the nineties, product was king. But in the twenty-first century, packaging is God. Surround anyone with glamour, glitz, gossip, controversy, sleaze, and you can make them a star. Case in point: The Kardashians— the epitome of current pop-culture values—'famous for being famous'.

I understand this phenomenon better than most. I've actually done it. I've made superstars out of very ordinary people. I didn't set out to do it, it wasn't my passion or aim, but I simply found myself guiding people towards celebrity status. I also found out I was really f?@king good at it. They didn't have to be intelligent, creative, or even talented. They just had to be 'not ugly' and have enough money.

Fame is all about the media. And the media is for sale. When I started creating personal brands a decade ago, you could, discreetly, buy a story on Page Three. Now, you can buy stories in the entertainment, sports, business and domestic news sections. Headlines are designed, or at least prioritized on the basis of their entertainment quotient. It was about five years ago that

I realized that 40 per cent of our daily news is dedicated to building the brands of personalities and social icons, rather than to actual journalism.

I don't blame the celebrities; they are just catering to the demands of the consumers. The crowds demand them. The masses consume them. They lust after larger-than-life personas. The general public aspires to someday be as famous as these personas. They want their every move to be watched, their every action documented, their photo to appear in the tabloids every few days. They just don't have enough money to buy it. Or, if they do have enough money, they're not exactly sure how to spend it to get the desired result—notoriety.

I've seen many a newly rich gentleman spend a shitload of money on a pompous, seven-star party with a socialite-only guest list. He was hoping to be photographed in their company, but found himself spliced out of every photo in the editing room. He spent his money on the Cristal and the caviar, but his guests wrote their cheques to the tabloids to ensure that their own photos were printed. The rich guy created an 'experience' and a chance for everyone else to show up on Page Three, but he didn't progress in establishing himself as a brand.

If you've got ten lakhs and two weeks, I can turn you into a decently recognizable brand. I would choreograph for you a unique and identifiable style, then buy a few strategically placed articles in several newspapers, secure some invites to the right parties, and introduce you to a few photojournalists who will guarantee that you continue to be noticed. I will give you the cue to walk the red carpet, teach you the right expressions to use at just the right moment, arrange a few guest appearances at a fashion show, and…voila! You are a society celebrity in India's commercial and entertainment capital!

Again, don't get me wrong. This is not the case for everyone that I have worked with. I had the good fortune of building brands like Aishwarya Rai, Hrithik Roshan, Saurav Ganguly, Kapil Dev, Yuvraj Singh and Vijender Singh, just to name a few. Really talented people who worked their asses off and truly deserve the iconic status that they have achieved. And lots of talented people that I haven't worked with, also: no one can deny that Shah Rukh Khan has been completely dedicated to giving his audience what it wants; Katrina Kaif has put in tremendous time and effort to learn Hindi; Vidya Balan got fat for a role.

My question is, when you open the newspapers, how come you don't read about V. S. Ramachandran's fascinating discoveries about the human brain? Why aren't parties thrown to celebrate Seshadri Srinivasan, the then seventy-seven-year-old architect who designed the Mumbai Sea Link in 2009, or for Tasneem Mehta, who conceptualized, curated, designed and implemented the restoration of the Dr Bhau Daji Lad Museum in Mumbai, or for R. K. Gupta, the project director for the Agni-V missile? Why aren't people like Sunita Williams, Indian-origin NASA astronaut, or Kulandei Francis, the social worker who, individually, rebuilt the lives of 1,53,990 women with a rural savings-and-credit group, walking the red carpet at the Filmfare Awards as celebrity guests?

Maybe it's because real achievers aren't interested in the kind of fame that Page Three offers. They probably wouldn't mind if the world knew their name, but I'm sure they could give a monkey if the press wrote about what brand of shoes they wear, when they change their hair colour and who they are dating.

But it's more likely that we, the general society, just aren't that interested in real achievers. We don't care about the content. It's the package that we want. It's the hype that gets our attention. The promotion. We worship the 'famous because they are famous' because it gives us hope that, even if we don't work hard for anything, even if we don't accomplish anything in this life, maybe we have a shot at being famous too—if we can just spin it the right way.

In a country driven by passion, tradition, and a unique culture, when did we forget to worship the real heroes?

F?@K IT LIST III
(YES, AGAIN.)

'I CANNOT GIVE YOU THE FORMULA FOR SUCCESS. BUT I CAN
GIVE YOU THE FORMULA FOR FAILURE—DON'T TRY.'

Sooooo…how are you coming along on that F?@k It List?

You thought I'd let it go by now, didn't you? I told you, it's not some abstract list. You should really, actually, do it. It will change your life. I won't say it again.

Since the time that you have had your ass and brains in place, you have been programmed by someone else—your parents, peers, friends. Do you really want to die, having only lived someone else's dream?

Do you even know what *your* dream is?

I was twenty-nine. I heard the sounds of my parents arguing through the window, before I opened the door to the house. It was such a heated argument that they didn't hear me come in and drop my cricket kit down on the floor.

'What's wrong? What happened? Why are you shouting?' I asked.

'Nothing, nothing, beta. Everything's fine,' my mum said.

'Big balls, it is!' I said.

Okay, I didn't actually say that to my parents. I said, 'Obviously it's not all fine. Why don't you tell me what's going on?'

Long story short—it had suddenly dawned on them that after

living for sixty and fifty-five years each, they hadn't really lived a single moment for themselves. One of them had blamed the other for an unfulfilled dream, and the other had countered with blame for an unfulfilled dream of their own. Because they had gone on for so many years, wanting something, but not making it happen, the volume of the discussion had quickly risen to match the intensity of the longing and regret they felt.

'What are these dreams that you haven't been able to fulfil?' I asked.

'Oh, you know, just things,' my mum said.

'Wait, wait...' I jumped up and grabbed a pen and paper—you know how I feel about writing things down! 'This is serious stuff, mum. I have just two questions: Who are you? And what do you want?'

'Oh, I'm not playing these games! This is not a quiz contest. This is a serious discussion between your father and I.'

'Please, mum, just do it. You too, dad. Tell me, I'll write it down for you.'

Mum went first: 'I am the devoted wife of Mr Mangal Singh, mother of my beautiful children, and grandmother to their growing brood. And, while I am satisfied and happy in being these things, there are just a few things that I feel I have earned after all these years. I want exactly $1,000 a month, in my bank account, to be able to use however I wish, whether to spend, donate or gift, to whomever I want, without having to ask for permission. Also, I want the keys to an independent, two-bedroom flat. I love my children, but, sometimes you all are completely unbearable and I want a quiet place of my own to be able to run to, when you lot are troubling me. I may never go there, but I need to know that it is there for me. And I want a five-carat diamond.'

Dad listened patiently, and then spoke: 'I am a devoted husband, father and grandfather, an accomplished and retired sugar technologist. I am proud of the life I have lived. I want only for my family to be happy.'

'Dad...' I said. 'There must be something, a little more specific, that you want.'

'Well, your mother and I have always wanted to go to Amsterdam and see the tulips in full bloom. We also wanted to see The Hague. And, I want to see my eldest grandson graduate from Harvard.'

When they finished listing their wants, I put the pencil down, looked at them, and said, 'Well, this is all very doable, isn't it?'

Within four months, we, together, fulfilled everything on the list. My mother was right, after so many years of putting up with all of us, she deserved a place to escape to. She had earned her right to spend her money as she saw fit, for being a devoted wife, mother and grandmother, and she also deserved a pretty, sparkly diamond. When spring rolled across Europe, we packed the entire family and went to see the tulips bloom across Amsterdam. We visited The Hague. Within a few months, my nephew had been accepted at Harvard. Unfortunately, my father passed before my nephew graduated, but I know that he was there with us, standing proud, on that special day.

If that story doesn't convince you to finally sit down, figure out who you are and what you want out of life, then...well, I'm going to try just one more thing.

I know that it's not easy to take out a piece of paper and write a letter to yourself. It feels a little dumb. Like writing an assignment for school. So, instead of writing down the answers to these two simple questions—Who are you? And what do you want?—for you to read back to yourself, why don't you write them down and send them across to me? I'm a cool dude. I've written a book. It's like you're writing to a kick-ass penpal.

Send me your answer to these two questions, at: ssfckknows@gmail.com

I won't judge. I won't even comment on your responses. I will simply keep your letter filed away nicely, and then…mail it back to you in six months time. It will remind you that, once upon a time, not so long ago, you actually took the first step to start living life for yourself. You will either have the opportunity to feel proud that you are making decisions each and every day to live up to your true self. Maybe you will feel like a total f?@king superstar if you have accomplished all of your goals. Or maybe you will feel like a total f?@king loser that you didn't accomplish any of them at all.

F?@k knows when you will find someone else who cares about you enough to do this for you!

PEACOCK IN THE FOREST

Pop Quiz: You have twenty seconds to answer the following question...

Question: We've talked about understanding who you are and what you want out of life, listening to your heart, following your gut, the F?@k It List, journeys, destinations and fate. What is the ultimate objective of all our discussions?

Your time starts...now!

Doo doo doo dada doo doo doo, doo doo doo doo DOO doodoodoodoodoo doo doo doo dada doo doo doo, DUH duhduhduh duh DUH duh.

Think you got it? I hope so. If you haven't been able to answer this question by now, then I've wasted a few good months writing it all out for you.

The answer is:

We are doing this so that you can make the most of your short life, by living it your way, on your terms. Your desires are inborn, and your heart and gut will show you the way, if you listen. This is the formula for happiness.

We are working on all this so that you can find happiness, shithead! Was that your answer? Good, you've understood.

However, there is one more aspect to this whole journey of self-discovery and self-belief that we haven't talked about yet.

It's one of the most exciting aspects of the whole journey, but I didn't want you f?@kers to get too excited and jump the gun, so I'm discussing it only now.

There's an old Indian saying: 'Jungle mein mor nacha, kisne dekha?'

Translated literally, it means: 'Peacock danced in forest, who saw?'

Translated figuratively, it means: 'There is no point being a peacock that dances in the forest if there is no one around to see.'

What is the point of having all those beautiful feathers and all those ostentatious dance moves, if you dance in the forest with no one around to appreciate it all?

Now, for the peacock it's probably fine, because it's not vain. It doesn't care to impress anyone but the peahen, who would presumably be there in the forest with him. But if you take this saying figuratively, then you will realize that there is a very good point to be made here.

It really is all about being happy, but...it's also great to be able to show the world what you have accomplished. I can give you a whole bunch of gyaan about how your personal successes should be shared only to inspire others to succeed in their own lives. But, really, we both know that it's all about showing off.

All those little assholes who used to tease you in school and tell you that you were a loser and would always be one; how fun is it to go back to your reunion and tell them that you are the world-class dietician that you had always aspired to be (proven by your international bestselling books, *What Goes In Must Come Out*, *The Glass Jar Experiment* and *The Sugar Technologist's Son's Teeth*). How about telling all those girls who thought you were 'boring', that you hiked through the Grand Canyon, saved a man from drowning in the Dead Sea (because it is possible to drown in its salty waters, contrary to popular belief), and learned to fly a helicopter?

Or your parents, who used to tell you that you couldn't make a career out of sport; how fun is it to be known as the Sports Marketing Guru of India, crack the biggest sports sponsorship in the country, and at forty-six, still win the man-of-the-match title in the summer cricket league in the UK?

It feels damn good to show off. No one is going to celebrate your triumphs for you. You have to blow your own horn. You work very hard, cross milestones, achieve brilliant things, succeed where others have failed, but if you do not manage to communicate this in the public domain nobody will know you and nobody will celebrate you.

This is actually an age-old sponsorship principal; if you buy an event or a property for a hundred dollars, you should have another hundred dollars in your pocket to let the world know that you own that event or property. Similarly, your extraordinary efforts should not just end with success; you must put equal effort in letting the world know what you did.

The world loves people who succeed. You just have to lobby your successes. Package and market your achievements, so that people don't have to work too hard to appreciate you. You have to be a bit arrogant if you want today's society to respect you.

That's how a few people have done it here in Bollywood. One of them is a young, upcoming actress who hasn't been in any box-office hit movies, and has still become famous. She's just done lots of hair commercials, fashion shoots and Page Three appearances with a posture that states: 'You should love me.' And the country has fallen for it.

Tell them enough that they should love you, and they eventually will. However, unless you've done something to earn it, they will forget about you as soon as the next pretty package comes along. If you earn respect by being true to who you are, and accomplishing what makes you the most happy, then who can blame you for a little—okay, totally flamboyant—boasting now and then?

I DON'T BUY IT

'I HAVE AN AFFAIR WITH EVERY WOMAN I MEET.
THEY JUST DON'T KNOW ABOUT IT.'

A few years ago, I spent an absolutely charming evening polishing off a few bottles of wine with a very powerful bureaucrat. There is no way that I can divulge his name, so don't even ask...

As the Pinot Noir kicked in, the conversation heated up.

I asked him, 'Hey bro, can you make love to someone you don't love?'

He said, 'Dude, for sure. I don't need love. It's purely carnal for me. It's fulfilling a biological need. Finding a much-desired physical release.'

I said, 'Doesn't it feel odd to you? Putting your tongue down a stranger's throat, swapping spit, exchanging bodily fluids, just for a moment of release?'

'Oh, I don't kiss them.'

'Just like Julia Roberts?'

'What?'

'Never mind. So, you've never been in love?'

'Sure, I have. But, basically,' he said, 'I don't buy anything that flies, sails or f?@ks. I rent it. The cost of parking it is more than the cost of using it.'

In case I couldn't figure it out for myself, he explained. 'It costs more to park a plane in the hanger, than to fly it. It costs more to dock a ship in the harbour, than to sail it.'

And, in case I was too stupid to see where this was going, he enlightened me further. 'For just eleven minutes of pleasure a day, it is very expensive to park a woman for twenty-three hours and forty-nine minutes at home. Or in your heart, for that matter. It's terribly expensive and terrifically painful.'

Remember kids, not everyone who is older is wiser. My bureaucrat friend believes himself to be contemporary and clever. But if you want to know the truth, my guess is that he has never really been in love.

F?@K BUDDIES

'FRIENDS FOREVER.
SEX NEVER.'

I first learned about this concept while watching *L.A. Law*. For you youngsters, *L.A. Law* was a TV serial that we all used to watch in the nineties. The nineties is not that long ago, f?@ker.

The show revolved around two very aggressive lawyers—one male, one female. They were partners in the same firm, each with very ambitious agendas. They worked, tirelessly, day and night to achieve their targets, and were left with no time for personal relationships outside of work. But, in an effort to accommodate their unrelenting biological needs, they decided that every Wednesday evening they would meet in one or the other's house, and pretend to be a 'normal' couple. They would share a bottle of wine, make sweet talk, and then gently f?@k each other's brains out. They came up with a compromise in which they were not deprived of love and sex, but were able to avoid the agony and consumption of time that comes with a normal relationship. 'F?@k buddies' is totally mainstream now, and I find it damn amusing.

'Introducing the latest and greatest in human relationships: "F?@k buddies"! No time? No foreplay required! Do it without emotions. Do it for a cause!'

You might not believe this, but...personally, I find it

inconceivable to share bodily fluids with someone that I'm not in a relationship with. Call me old-fashioned, I just can't stomach it. To put your tongue into some stranger's mouth, bite their waxy earlobes, roll your tongue down the crack of their butt... the thought makes me nauseous. Even when I'm totally smashed, the thought of sucking on some random's toes makes me want to vomit.

You kids want everything pre-packaged these days. On demand. Instant...like your coffee. Just add hot water, stir and sip.

I can't do it that way. It takes away all the fun. I like to be able to grind my beans just right. Not too coarse, not too fine. I love when the aroma fills the whole kitchen as it brews. I love the anticipation of waiting to take that first sip and see if I got all the elements just right.

You settle for Nescafe. You have fun making love on Skype and f?@king each other on BBM. I just can't give up the feeling of the flesh and lips of a woman that I am madly in love with. I know that there is nothing that I can do to convince you. But I am 100 per cent positive that you'll figure it out later, when you finally and ultimately fall in love.

Now don't get me wrong. I'm not the brand ambassador for *Romeo and Juliet* or anything. I'm a 'live and let live' kind of guy. Whatever floats your boat. Whatever blows your skirt up.

What I'm trying to tell you is that, you may not know it yet, but there is absolutely nothing that compares to being in love. I'm giving you something to look forward to.

Being f?@k buddies is the trendy thing right now, but, if you look closely at all the films and shows based on it, *No Strings Attached*, *Friends with Benefits*, *Sex and the City*: season two, episode fourteen (not that I would know about that one), they all end the same way. The sex is never enough. They either fall head over heels in love with each other, albeit reluctantly, due to some previous daddy issues or lingering heartbreak, or, like Carrie Bradshaw, realize that the sex is empty and meaningless and call it off to go in search of the real thing (at least that's what someone told me she did).

You're young, your hormones are screaming, and it may seem like a good f?@k buddy is all you need, but, just like in the movies, one day, you'll find someone you truly love. You'll want to walk off into the sunset hand-in-hand with them.

You can either bonk all your juices out until then, or you can save that very precious part of yourself, for that very special person.

SEX VS LOVE:
THE CHEESECAKE EXPERIMENT

'I LOVE WOMEN WITH NAMES LIKE SHEILA, MUNNI AND
CHAMELI. THEY SOUND LIKE BEAUTIFUL FLOWERS.'

I think that sex is reasonably overrated. Orgasms are great,
no doubt. But, I'm all about the anticipation. The better the
foreplay, the better the orgasm. And by foreplay, I don't just mean
a little nibble on the neck and the obligatory thirty seconds spent
on her breasts before you stick it in.

I mean the chase. The whole f?@king hunt. The first eye
contact. The batting of her eyelashes. Finding an excuse to bump
into her and say 'Hi'. A few words exchanged, a quick glance over
her shoulder before she leaves for the night, without giving you
her number. The dressing up, the hairstyling, visiting the same
club every Friday night, hoping to see her again. No luck. And
then, bam! You see her again at the opening night of the new
club just down the block. More flirting. More batting eyelashes.
Numbers exchanged. Dinner. Movie. Drinks. Dinner. Movie.
Drinks. Dinner. Art gallery. Drinks. Her house. (The art gallery
does it every time.)

That is foreplay. When you have worked so hard to get it,
when you've really earned it, after dreaming about it for so long,
that orgasm is so much more frickin' fun. It's not like orgasms
are tough to come by. You don't even need any props or tools,

just a quiet room and a hand. The fun is not in the release, it's all in the build-up.

You may find this rather cheesy (pun intended), but I have an analogy to illustrate this. (Did you catch that? That's two literary terms in one sentence. I'm getting the hang of this whole writing thing.)

Close your eyes and pick your favourite dessert. Your absolute favourite, sugary, sweet dessert...as long as it's cheesecake.

This is a comparative analogy. So, in the first case, let's imagine that you are sitting in your office around teatime, waiting for your next out of a dozen meetings to happen, and your secretary comes in with a piece of blueberry cheesecake. She puts it down in front of you and says, 'For you, sir.' And you say, 'Hey, that's really nice. Thanks.' And she just stands there smiling and you say, 'Umm, thanks for...bringing me the cake, because...' And her smile fades and she says, 'It's my birthday, sir. I wrote it on your calendar. Next year I'll leave a post-it note on your desk.' And she walks out.

She immediately calls you to inform you that your four-thirty meeting is waiting in the boardroom. The cheesecake looks damn good, and you are hungry because you rushed your lunch, again. So you quickly devour the cheesecake. It tastes pretty decent and the rush of sugar gets you a little high. You wash it down with some stale coffee and throw away the paper plate. On the way out, you tell your secretary 'thank you' again, but not 'Happy Birthday', because you are too embarrassed that you forgot, and head to the boardroom. In the boardroom, in the middle of your meeting you crash from the sugar rush. By the time you walk out of the boardroom, the cheesecake is totally forgotten and you are looking for your next sugar fix.

Good fun, huh? A surprise cheesecake delight thrown in on

an otherwise hectic day. Woo-hoo.

Now, here's the second case. You stare out the window of your office, watching the monsoon clouds hide the tops of the tallest buildings. You get a tingle in your tummy, and a slice of cheesecake appears behind your eyelids every time you blink. You start daydreaming about your favorite kind... Baked, or unbaked? Ricotta or cream cheese? With a dollop of whipped cream on top, or warm blueberry sauce? Your mouth starts to water.

You try to remember when it was that you had it last. You remembering saying: 'Mmmmmmmm. This is like eating a slice of heaven!' Where was that? Where do you get the best cheesecake around here? If you don't remember, you ask your friends if they remember. Or maybe you go on Zomato and read some reviews. While browsing the reviews you see a snapshot of a café, and instantly realize that that's the one! That's where you had that last perfect slice. You decide that tomorrow, after work, you are going to that restaurant for cheesecake. You make a reservation, just to be safe. It's the last thing you think about before you fall asleep that night. You have a date with a slice of heaven tomorrow.

As the hours at work tick by the next day, all you think about is that cheesecake. You eat a very light lunch, so that your oesophagus and stomach are clean and ready for that fluffy, bliss-inducing cake made of cheese. No acid reflux, no bile burps to ruin the delicate flavour.

You finish your emails, lock your office, tell your driver where to go and follow the route in your mind's eye, guessing how many more minutes before you reach. Before you are seated, you go to the dessert counter and look at the perfectly shaped, pale yellow masterpiece. They've sliced the cake with utmost precision, but there is one piece that looks just a little bit more perfect than the rest. You tell the waiter, *that* is the piece you would like. That piece is yours.

You sit down at the table, catch a whiff of something strange, and realize that you are seated right next to the loo. No good. You request to be moved to the recently vacated table by the window. Why should you compromise? Today, it is all about you. And the cheesecake.

The restaurant is playing the Bee Gees, which really doesn't fit with the French café theme that they are trying to pull off. And it wasn't what you imagined would be playing when you ate your cheesecake. You request them to please change the music. 'Oh, you don't have any other CDs? Why don't you plug in my iPod? I'm sure no one will object to some Norah Jones.'

Table in the window, Norah Jones, and the perfect slice of cheesecake in front of you. You pick up your fork, pausing just long enough for dramatic effect, take a deep breath and slide the fork through the tip of the cheesecake. You cut off a perfect little triangle.

Now, if you haven't realized where we're going with this analogy, then, well...you might not be the sharpest tool in the shed. So I'll spell it out for you. The first analogy, the cake just falling into your lap and needing to be eaten in a hurry, was a metaphor for casual sex. Easily attained, briefly satisfying, but an overall unmemorable and shallow experience that only leaves you wanting more.

The second analogy, with its anticipation and attention to environmental and emotional details, represents wooing, waiting, falling in love and then making love. We were just getting to the making love part...

You take that perfectly sliced little triangle and set it gently on your tongue. Your mouth starts to water as your taste buds come alive with that first rush of sugar. This is how you would kiss, very gently, the woman that you have been waiting so desperately for. Savouring her—her smell, her taste…wanting to treasure the moment forever.

You shut your eyes, let it linger in your mouth for some time—the cheesecake/her saliva. Once it's melted and softened, you swallow hard. Since you ate light food at lunch/have not had sex for a really long time, you will feel every part of that cheesecake sliding down into your stomach/every touch, everywhere on your body.

Since you have waited so long, and prepared so well, you will take your time to enjoy it/her. Taste every bite/kiss every inch of her. Feel the different textures of the cheese, the crust/her skin, her lips. You see just how long you can leave a bite/her on your tongue before it melts. Notice how perfectly the warm, wet blueberry sauce drips down the side of the cake/her legs feel. You see how long you can resist before you finally take that very last, perfect, ecstatic mouthful…

Isn't it amazing? That longed for, lusted after and slowly consumed cheesecake. It satisfies your hunger, your desire for the sweetest and richest things that this world has to offer. It's a small taste of what makes life worth living. It will be remembered fondly and you will look forward to the next time.

It's so much better than some knock-off cheesecake, made with cheese-flavoured pudding mix instead of real cheese, picked up last minute at the convenience store, eaten in a rush before your wife comes home and catches you breaking your diet. The one that you'll regret in the morning.

Don't accept substitutes for the real thing. Life is too short for compromise.

ORGASM AS CHARACTER STUDY

'*THEY* SAY THAT SEX IS BAD.
WELL, WE HAVE 1.24 BILLION INDIANS ON THE PLANET,
SO IT CAN'T BE *THAT* BAD.'

Think fast. What is the best feeling in the entire world? The correct answer is: an orgasm. That's what you were thinking, right? If you were thinking of something else, like laying your head on a cold pillow, holding a kitten in your lap, or eating ice cream, well then... You're obviously still a virgin, or have been married way too long.

Orgasms are the most amazing feeling ever. Every nerve in your body gets activated, every single muscle tenses up in anticipation and you can feel the blood rushing through your veins when you release. It's blissful.

But more than the physical feeling of the release, the true beauty of an orgasm is that your brain shuts off for a few incredible moments. Your ceaseless, relentless mind shuts the f?@k up! It's the closest most of us can come to nirvana without living in a cave in the Himalayas, meditating and fasting all day.

And—bonus!—you lose six hundred calories every time you have an orgasm! That's, like, better than two hours running on the treadmill, and soooo much more fun. The trick is that you have to surrender to the orgasm. You have to give in to the pleasure, and you have to scream in ecstasy.

If you simply grunt a few times and let out a little whimper at the end, then you are doing yourself more harm than good. You are repressing your true feelings, and not allowing your energies and juices to flow free! You'll end up with ruptured balls or a popped vein somewhere, trust me.

They say that you can truly judge a man's character by the way he behaves on the sports field and in the bedroom. (Similarly, you can judge a woman's true character by the way she acts while shopping and in the bedroom.) These are the up close and personal, high-level performance arenas. With a little competition and something at stake, a man's true colours are sure to shine through.

Over the years, I've been properly introduced to many a man on the cricket field. But, for some strange reason, I have also found myself witness to the bedroom behaviour of not one, but two of my very close friends.

It wasn't by choice, mind you. You think I want to see another man have sex? F?@k no.

I, for sure, can't share their names, but I can entertain you with their stories. The first one was an older friend, sixty-two years old, but damn strong. We were travelling for an event, and booked in a suite at the best five-star hotel in the city. To get to my room at the end of the night, I had to pass by his. His door was ajar, and I just pushed it open a little bit more, to say a quick goodnight. I caught him on top of a pretty brunette, just about to explode into orgasm. I was stunned for a moment, but then decided to stick around and see how he expressed himself in that moment. How could I not take advantage of this opportunity to get a glimpse into his character, which I would never otherwise get a chance to see?

As he picked up speed, his deep groans grew into manly

grunts, but as he reached the pinnacle of his pleasure, he clamped his mouth shut, ground his teeth together and growled like a constipated grizzly bear. A really guttural, painful sounding 'grrrrrRRRMmmm!'

It was so freaking hilarious, I laughed out loud. He ducked under the covers to hide, and avoided me the next day. But now, every time I see him, I don't say, 'Hi. What's up?' I say, 'grrrrrRRRMmmm!'

Because I teased him so much about that night, and that sound, one sunny day on the golf course, he decided to explain himself to me. He told me that, just a week prior to that 'encounter', he had a minor surgery. He was advised to avoid physical stress and 'loud expression' (for real, they told him to be as quiet as possible). He couldn't resist the temptation of a little physical stress and an orgasm, but he did try his best to control the expression of it!

The second character study was absolutely forced upon me. I was just falling asleep in my hotel room, after a long day of meetings and presentations at a business conference. My dear friend and temporary roommate came in, stinking of vodka, with some random chick on his arm. 'Oh, f?@k,' I heard him say. 'He's already here.' I kept my eyes jammed shut and pretended to be asleep. I wasn't about to be kicked out of my comfy bed for his four minutes of fun.

'Let's go,' she said.

'No, no,' he replied. 'There's nowhere else to go.'

'I'm not doing it with him here,' she whispered. Somehow, through magical powers instilled in him by vodka, he convinced the shy girl to crawl into his bed, not six feet away from mine. Ah, there's nothing like the rustling sound of two bodies molesting each other under the covers, trying to be quiet about it.

After the obligatory few minutes, the long strokes of heavy petting stopped and the rhythmic rocking started. She was being incredibly quiet, but he started grunting softly. I tried to block the breathy sounds by burying my head under the pillow, but he just got louder and louder.

After a while, I heard him say, 'Say my name.'

She was quiet.

'Say my name!' he said again.

No response.

'Say...my...NAME!' he shouted.

'WHAT *IS* YOUR NAME?' she shouted back.

F?@K KNOWS WHY RIGHT IS WRONG AND WRONG IS RIGHT

'PROSTITUTION IS LEGAL IN THAILAND. DRUGS ARE ALLOWED IN AMSTERDAM. CORRUPTION IS THE CENTRAL POINT OF THE NEW ECONOMY OF INDIA. TERRORISM THE MOST PROFITABLE BUSINESS IN THE WORLD. F?@K WHAT'S RIGHT. F?@K WHAT'S WRONG.'

There is no such thing as right and wrong. Right becomes wrong and wrong becomes right depending on the point of view of the person who is either preaching or living it.

The same political party that is 'wrong' today and voted out of power, becomes 'right' tomorrow and voted back in. Is it right to drive on the right side of the road, like the UK and India? Or is it right to drive on the left side of the road, like in the US and France? Is it right to take out student loans and be in debt for fifteen years, to get a degree in business science or economics? Or is it right to drop out of school and start your own business, like Bill Gates?

Is it right to believe in science? The evolutionary theory of science says that the whole purpose of life is to procreate and assumes the truth of the survival of the fittest. Should we believe this? Why does cancer happen? Is it because of wi-fi or mobile signals filtering through our brains? No one wants to explain to you why the interference from the phone makes the radio shift.

Imagine what it is doing to your brainwaves. Is it healthy to keep talking on the mobile?

We know 'tobacco kills', but yet smoking is shown in movies all the time. We know alcoholism is a massive problem around the world, but yet 90 per cent of Hollywood movies and cable networks show actors pouring themselves a whisky at 10 a.m. Because Indian laws forbid the advertisement of alcohol in media, the industry embeds it into your entertainment experience through sponsorships. Doesn't that just seem wrong?

For most people, it's not about emotions, it's about economics. And economics blurs the line between right and wrong. We are willing to risk health, safety and security for financial prosperity. We are willing to reap the rewards now, without worrying about the effects of our actions on the next generation.

Red wine is good, and then red wine is bad. Lalit Modi was a respected businessman and now he's a fugitive. It's confusing as hell.

So to summarize, there is no right and there is no wrong. Wrong can become right, if you make a decision to do it with conviction and self-confidence. Right can become wrong, if you stand in someone else's shoes. That's what your entire journey of life is—'the art of drawing sufficient conclusions from insufficient premises,' as Samuel Butler said. No media outlet can do that for you. You have to consider your premises and decide for yourself what is right and what is wrong.

FUCK KNOWS IF GREED ISN'T ACTUALLY GOOD

'GREED, FOR LACK OF A BETTER WORD, IS GOOD. GREED IS RIGHT. GREED WORKS. GREED CLARIFIES, CUTS THROUGH, AND CAPTURES THE ESSENCE OF THE EVOLUTIONARY SPIRIT. GREED, IN ALL OF ITS FORMS: GREED FOR LIFE, FOR MONEY, FOR LOVE, KNOWLEDGE, HAS MARKED THE UPWARD SURGE OF MANKIND AND GREED, YOU MARK MY WORDS, WILL NOT ONLY SAVE TELDAR PAPER, BUT THAT OTHER MALFUNCTIONING CORPORATION CALLED THE USA.'

–GORDON GEKKO, *WALL STREET*

I have to confess, when Michael Douglas, as Gordon Gekko, gives his speech about greed being good, it was one of the most exciting moments for me in cinema. I watched the film in London and to this day, I'm not sure if it was Douglas's conviction, or the dialogue itself, but I believed him! It's not an exaggeration, and I'm not too proud to admit that from that day forward, I was convinced that greed was indeed good.

Of course, the word 'greed' has many dark meanings to it. But if you remain optimistic about the idea, then 'greed' is simply wanting more out of life. Wanting more out of your job, wanting more out of your creativity, and wanting more for yourself. That isn't such a bad thing. In my professional career, whenever I wanted more out of circumstances or situations, I got more, but as a result, I was also able to share and give more to more people.

My company was rocking, but I wanted more projects, more clients, more profits, and so I hired more people. I now have over a thousand employees who earn salaries and who advance in their career, because I wanted more. I threw lots of parties, but I wanted to throw a bigger party, so I created Sunburn. Now, more than one lakh people get to party here every year. How is that bad?

Nothing is inherently good or bad in this world. It's all about the choices that we make.

'They say the colour of money is important.
That's why it's got three colours.
Black money, white money and grey money.'

HIMMAT-E-MARDA
MADAD-E-KHUDA

'I TRIED...I TRIED AGAIN...AND THEN
I STARTED TO CELEBRATE TRYING.'

There's an Urdu saying, 'Himmat-e-marda madad-e-Khuda', which means: 'The bravery of man is supported by the grace of God'. Basically, it says that, if your effort is sincere and your commitment inexhaustible, then God will support you in your endeavour. In translation, it also means that 'there is God in effort'. If you are trying, then you are on the godly path, and that—more than success—is what truly matters.

There are two ways of seeing this.

The first is to believe that following the godly path is what matters in the end. To believe that what matters in this life is to listen to your heart, hear what it wants, where it wants to go, and go out and make that happen to the best of your abilities.

It doesn't matter if you want to broker world peace or build the world's largest popsicle-stick castle. It doesn't matter if you want to save an endangered species, or run a small juice shack in Goa. If you approach something—anything—sincerely and with 100 per cent in your mind, heart and spirit, then you are truly living your life.

And if you are sincere, if you are truly dedicated in your efforts, you are bound to succeed. It may not happen the first time. It may not happen the second time. But you will eventually be rewarded for your efforts. If you alone can't make it happen, with your own hands, then God will notice all your effort and step in to give you a hand. He will send you some big idea, a new client, or some inheritance. Your dedication to your task is like a prayer to God. He will hear you. He will help you. He won't allow someone so sincere to falter.

That's a lovely thought, isn't it? I would love to live by that idea. As the joint managing director of India's first, and only, entertainment, media and communication conglomerate, I should value the effort of my employees. If they are perfectly clear about what they want and understand what it is that I want them to do, and they try really, really hard to get it, then I should be pleased. If they don't meet their numbers in one month, I shall give them four more months to bring in that amount, as long as I see them trying hard. If they don't close that big account, then I shall give them three more to try and close it. If they are working sincerely, then I shall be proud of them.

And the best part is, if people are working sincerely towards their goals, regardless of the outcome, they are happy people. Their own effort makes them happy. I like to have happy people around me. I like to have happy people in my company. If people are happy and keep trying, then success will come, eventually. I can wait.

The second way is to say 'big balls!' to the idea. The godly path matters more than success? Really? Losers are as good as winners, as long as they have tried hard? Really?

I mean, are you kidding me? Success doesn't matter? How many bestselling biographies have you read about people who try really, really hard in life, but ultimately end up failing in their endeavours? Walt Disney became a household name because he created Disney, not because he was fired from his newspaper job and went bankrupt after unsuccessfully launching a number of start-ups. You wouldn't have read about Thomas Edison's one thousand unsuccessful attempts at inventing the light bulb, if attempt number 1001 hadn't actually worked. We don't write books about the losers. Mistakes are not learnings. They are just failures.

How many fairy tales do you read to your kids where the prince rides all through the kingdom, having damsels try on the glass slipper, but never, ever finds his Cinderella? Are you telling me what matters is that the prince finds happiness in following his haphazard plan, while Cinderella languishes locked away in the attic? We don't build statues to 'that guy who fought super long and super hard to save the black rhinoceros, but failed'. The Fortune 500 list does not give a special mention to 'that guy who worked ridiculously long hours, neglecting his family, in order to fulfil his dream of becoming a Fortune 500 CEO, but was only able to become vice-president of his local Walmart.'

We reward successes. Is God any different? What is God's role in all of this?

Dinosaurs surely fought really hard to stay alive. I bet you they gave their continuing existence their full and undivided attention. How did that work out for them? How about that guy who wanted nothing more than to climb to the top of Mt Everest but is now frozen, with his backpack still on, somewhere on the mountainside? He didn't go up there half-assed, for sure. God didn't seem to notice his sincerity, nor reward it with a nice gentle descent back home to his family to celebrate.

You watch a cart puller, pulling a cart piled high with luggage through the busiest intersection in Mumbai, and you can see the amount of effort he is putting in. He's eighty years old, bowlegged, and sweating heavily in the forty-five-degree heat. He's pulled that cart for the last seventy years, giving it his best, every day of his life.

Just near by, in the high-rise building, there are a hundred CEOs, sitting in air-conditioned boardrooms, drinking their cappuccinos and making decisions about other people's money. Have those CEOs worked harder than that cart puller? Have they been more sincere in their efforts? Are they more deserving of success? I'm not convinced. Is the cart puller the happiest person in the city, because he puts in most effort? I highly doubt it.

As the joint managing director of India's first, and only, entertainment, media and communications conglomerate, success is the only acceptable way forward. I value the success of my employees. They have profit and loss expectations. If they don't succeed in what they set out to do, or what I have sent them out to do, then how can I justify the expenses to keep them on the payroll? Do you know that the building maintenance, air conditioning, training and benefits all added up costs double that person's salary to keep them sitting at their desk? They may put in the most hours, visit the most clients, make more pitches than anyone else, but, if they don't close that sale, if they don't get that big account, well then, I have to free up my infrastructure for someone who can. In work, as in life, there is no budget set aside to reward 'good effort'.

Nothing succeeds like success.

I'D RATHER HAVE THEM LAUGH WITH ME WHILE I'M ALIVE, THAN CRY FOR ME WHEN I DIE

'WHEN YOU ARE BORN, EVERYBODY IS LAUGHING AND YOU ARE CRYING. WHEN YOU DIE, EVERYBODY IS CRYING, SO YOU HAD BETTER BE LAUGHING.'

Of late, I have noticed a very disturbing trend—more people will come to your funeral, than ever came to all your birthday parties combined. It's harder to get a guest list going for a wedding anniversary than for your dad's condolence meeting. In the current age of economy-ruled emotions, if you invite a hundred people to come and celebrate a joyful moment, you'll be lucky if ten of them show up. But the minute you tell them that you've had a death in the family, or that you've got an illness that could lead to your death, you practically get a standing ovation.

It's not that people have turned to the dark side and only want to celebrate death. There is just no f?@king time to celebrate other people's happiness and success, while you are trying to create your own. It's kind of obligatory for you to spend some‑ time on condolences and sympathy, otherwise you'll be labelled a 'cold-hearted bitch/bastard'. But celebrations are totally optional.

I know this better that anyone. In running such a massive event-management business, my office once calculated that, on average, I was required to make an appearance at an event 290 nights out of the year. That was just for my own company's events! F?@k, man. If anyone else ever called me for their event, I would tell them, 'F?@k off! I need a rest!'

For the sake of my own work, I turned down lots and lots of invitations to celebrate with so many friends. But what happened was, when I started to reap the rewards of all my hard work and dedication, I had no friends left to come and celebrate with me. A pretty shitty catch-22.

By the time you start to realize what's happening, you've reached 'middle age'. Gone are the days of celebrating for the sake of celebrating, with the gang that you can always count on to rally at a moment's notice, or with welcoming, random strangers. At mid-life, a lot is dictated by protocol. If you want someone to come to the next event that you have planned, you indulge him and go to his event. If you want to 'seal the deal' with a new client, you go to his daughter's wedding and gift her a fat envelope of cash.

When I die, I don't want any of these idiots crying for me. F?@k that. I'd much rather be surrounded by people who will laugh with me while I am alive. Those people whom you call over from the next office and with whom you can spend two hours debating the new Sacha Baron Cohen film. ('Are you having a boy, or an abortion?') The ones whom, after a few bottles of red wine, you can convince to jump on the dining table and dance to some dirty Bollywood number. The ones who actually stop by your house to wish you a happy birthday, instead of sending you a text message.

In this respect, I'm a little jealous of my wife. She and her brood of sisters and cousins are absolutely inseparable. They stick with each other, through thick and thin, and are never lacking in support. But, even more than the blood bond, they are frickin' ridiculously happy people. Their love of life is completely infectious, and when they get together, nothing can stop them from bringing down the house with their laughter.

I want more people like that in my life, but they are damn hard to find.

When I think back to twenty years ago, when most of you were waddling around in diapers, I swear that I can recall the decibel level of general human chatter to be a hundred times louder than today. When you walked into a restaurant, a bar or a cinema, people were conversing with each other, giggling and laughing. People laughed with their neighbours, with the waitress, with strangers at the next table. There would be laughter emanating from around the corner or the phone booth in the lobby. In my memory, people were more…jolly.

With all the iPhones, iPods, iPads, BlackBerries and Dr Dre's Beatbox docks, people don't even look at each other any more, let alone smile and laugh. That's one of the reasons why 'laughter classes' have popped up all around the world. We've so forgotten the art of being happy that we have to pay someone to instruct us how to laugh!

'A moment of laughter is a moment of freedom.' I may have read that somewhere, or I might have made it up, I'm not sure. But wherever it came from, it's the absolute truth. Laughter is like an orgasm. The physical effects are mind-blowingly pleasurable, but orgasms and laughter are also mind-stopping.

For a few brief seconds, the mind surrenders to the intensity of genuine laughter, pauses its endless, egotistical tirade, and falls silent. That silence is breathtaking. That silence is the best sort of music you can possibly hear. I don't give a monkey about the moment of silence that they will observe for me at my funeral; I want perpetual, ecstatic laughter while I am alive.

GIVE, AND YOU SHALL RECEIVE

'LIFE IS SIMPLE—WHAT YOU GIVE IS WHAT YOU GET.'

When was the last time that you were greeted at the airport by your family after returning from a long journey? When was the last time that your best friend picked you up at the train station after a long absence? Do you remember that feeling? Has that ever even happened in your lifetime?

It's an amazing feeling. The sheer exhaustion, aches and pains from the trip being forgotten in the anticipation of being received by that person whom you had missed so much.

There's a brilliant montage at the end of the movie, *Love Actually*. Friends and family have come to Heathrow Airport to receive travellers from all around the world. Regardless of nationality, religion or age, the expressions on their faces are all the same—pure joy at meeting a loved one after so long. There are big hugs and even bigger smiles. It's an amazing feeling.

Whenever my father would have to travel on work, he would either go by the Indian Railways or the only airline in the country at the time, Indian Airlines. It was an event to drop him off and pick him up after his journey, something that we would never dream of missing.

At ten years of age, of course I loved seeing my father walking out of the airport terminal. But more than that, I loved the handful of candy that he would pull out of his pocket. He was a charming man, and it wasn't difficult for him to convince the stewardess to give him more than the two candies per passenger quota. Oh, how I used to hide those precious candies from my brothers and select just one a day to suck on. Life was so simple then. I gave him the joy of being missed and welcomed back home; he gave me sugar.

At the heart of it, we humans love those simple things. Warm hugs, strong handshakes, fond greetings, annual reunions. Friends dropping in for a cup of tea, surprise birthday parties, super-sized congratulations cards signed by everyone in the office. Being picked up at the airport.

We know how good these things feel. And we would love to have more of them in our lives. We hope for more of them. But how often are we willing to give them? You tell someone that you are going to miss them, but when was the last time you picked them up from the airport or station? You say that you are a good member of the community, but when was the last time you dropped in on a neighbour? You say you are kind and thoughtful, but when was the last time that you bought someone flowers or chocolate, just because? I bet it's been a while. There is always a meeting going on, or an errand to finish, or a happy hour to get to. There's always something else to do, isn't there?

We all say that we want to see a greener world. We all understand the significance of trees and plants and flowers. They give us oxygen. We need oxygen. We all whine that we live in a concrete jungle and that it is becoming more and more difficult to find a tree to sit under. But tell me, over the course of your life, how many trees have you planted? Have you planted even a single tree to make the world a greener place?

Stop whining about the concrete and go plant a tree. Stop saying that you miss her over the phone, stop giving your work priority over these precious moments. Actions speak louder than words. And it feels better to give than to receive. The more you give, I can assure you, the more you will get back. Just make sure that you pick up your gifts from duty free, because the airlines can't afford to give out candy any more.

F?@K ME,
I DON'T WANNA BE

'MOST PEOPLE NEVER GROW UP. THEY JUST GROW OLD.'

So, at this point in the book, have you been able to answer the two basic and most ultimate questions that I posed to you in the F?@k It List III chapter? (This is a follow-up on the follow-up...)

Do you walk around every day with the answers to those two important questions at the front of your mind? As the motivation for anything that you do? As the reason for everything that you do?

No? Why am I not surprised? Do you even remember the questions? Hmmm...

I'll reiterate:

Who are you?
And what do you want?

I really believe that if you can answer these two questions, confidently and honestly, then you are well on your way to a happy life and meaningful existence.

There is magic in knowing who you are, and what you want. The magic is that life suddenly becomes so bloody simple. Unf?@kingbelieveably simple. Take my word for it.

But I agree that it is not so easy to answer these questions. It took me about a year of answering, realizing that my answer wasn't fully accurate, changing my answer, testing it out, and realizing that wasn't quite right either, before I nailed it. That was a day to celebrate!

It can be daunting to jump straight to the big questions (although I have warmed you up a lot in this book). So, I'm going to share a secret with you...

Sometimes, in life, in order to find out what you want, it's easier to find out what you *don't* want, and work backwards. Find out who, for sure, you *don't* want to be, and then move a few steps closer to who it is you do want to be.

So, today, we are going to make a new list. The 'F?@k Me, I Don't Wanna Be' list!

Everything I have suggested to you in this book has been really very simple to do, although you never believe me. (You always do this to me!) This, is no exception. It's easy.

Just make a list of all the things that you, for sure, DON'T want to ever be. To make it even easier, I'll give you a sample of the most common responses:

F?@k Me, I Don't Wanna Be...

1.   Fat
2.   Broke
3.   Old
4.   Living in this dump
5.   In this loveless relationship
6.   Lonely
7.   Like my father
8.   In this stupid job
9.   Sick
10. Miserable any more

Now, you can work backwards. If you don't want to be fat, then take that fat ass of yours to the gym and get on the Stairmaster. If you don't want to be in a loveless relationship any more, then screw up your courage and tell your husband that you want to find someone with whom you can evolve. If you don't want to be lonely, then keep dragging out that loveless relationship until you find something better. Or break up and get a puppy.

Get it? Think you can handle this one? I do this all for your own good, you know.

Make your list, ponder over it, and the more things that you can identify that you don't want to be, the closer you will be to finding out:

Who you are.
And what you want.

Once you know those two things, there is absolutely nothing that can stop you from being happy.

ONE HOT JATT

'TO BE OR NOT TO BE. WHAT THE F?@K WAS THAT?'

Please note: the following chapter may offend the sensibilities of the very few distinguished and polished individuals who are reading this book. You may wish to skip to the next chapter.

Most of you, however, will enjoy this brief story.

I was fifteen. I had just come home from another long, gruelling day at school, full of academic struggles and teenage insecurities. I sat with my mother on the front porch of our house at the far end of our village, outside of Shamli, in Uttar Pradesh. My father wasn't expected home from the sugar mill for some time, so as my mum tossed and cleaned the rice for dinner, I laid all my troubles at her feet.

It was difficult to keep up with classes when all the words on the pages looked backwards and jumbled. Why couldn't I read as fast as the other kids? None of the girls wanted to be my partner in the science lab. Why couldn't I be fair and handsome like Rajesh Khanna? The cool guys were able to go to the movies every Friday night and wore denim jeans. I had only kurtas and shorts. Why couldn't I have been born to a rich family?

As my mother turned a deaf ear to my complaining, numbed by the years of listening to the same juvenile angst of my two older brothers, my uncle walked by.

He was strong, after a lifetime of tilling and toiling in the fields of his farm. He was powerful, after years of speaking his mind in the village council. He was well respected and intimidating in his dhoti, kurti and pagdi.

He stopped in his tracks as he heard my whining, 'Why couldn't I have been born into a famous family, and live in a mansion in New Delhi?'

My uncle stepped forward slowly and looked me dead in the eye. He raised his finger, wagged it at me, and in his blunt Haryanvi accent, said:

'Oye, puttar! Agar meri chachi ke pas lund hota to woh chacha hoti.'

For the English readers, roughly translated, this means:

'Oye, young boy. If my aunty had a penis, she would be called an uncle. But that is not possible, is it?'

I averted my eyes and meekly mumbled, 'Nahi hai, uncle. You're right. It's not possible.'

His statement, albeit rather crass, had quite an impact on me. No matter what I wanted to be, I was never going to be anything other than myself. I might as well start being happy living in my skin. I had my strengths and I had my weaknesses, but they were mine. I might as well be proud of them. Like I was proud of my lund.

I vowed to stop whining. Besides, what does whining accomplish, besides annoying everyone in earshot? It's not like there's a Bureau of Personal Characteristic and Cultural Identity Reassignment that could handle my case.

No one listens to your whining. And no one cares. F?@king accept what you have, and get on with your life.

Because of my uncle, who had no desire to be an aunty, I have learned to celebrate who I am. I am comfortable in my skin. I appreciate my heritage. The compensations that I make for my dyslexia have become strengths. My village roots have kept me grounded throughout my glitzy, glamorous life in Mumbai. The ladies seem to like my grizzly bear physique.

I wouldn't change a thing. I am one hot jatt.

BORN EQUAL

'TO F?@K IS PLEASURE. TO GET F?@KED IS NOT.'

We are born equal. We each have ten fingers, two eyes, two ears, one brain, one heart. It's the standard format. If for some reason, you have an extra thumb or an extra kidney or one less arm, then you are actually required by the government to register your 'deformity' on your personal identification documents. Apparently, you are still a human, but just a little misshapen.

As we grow, our DNA determines that this one has bigger breasts, that one has slanty eyes, the other one has giant feet, but those are just characteristics. Slight variations on the basic form. We are all of the same species. The same ancient extended family. We are all born brothers and sisters.

(I sometimes wonder who decides which branch of the family our soul gets placed into. Who decides that I'm going to be an Indian, and you a Chinese, and she an American. Is there a f?@king assembly line upstairs? Is there a technician who decides this lot will be born to the Japanese and the next few to the Swiss?)

We die equal. Unable to take anything from this life with us. No one leaves this life with any more, or any less than the next person. We are the same.

So why can't we all just get along?

There is so much conflict on the planet. Massive disagreements between countries, continents, races and political parties. Individuals constantly fighting with their neighbours. Religions fighting against other religions. From birth to life, in the middle, what causes all this conflict and confusion?

Is it geographical? Because you were born in the Western hemisphere, you should find fault with those born in the East? Is it the family to which you were born? If they are prejudiced against another race or people from other communities for some conflict they had long ago, should you also hate them? Is it the expectations of the society we grow up in, or the pressures and propaganda of our governments and religious leaders? F?@k knows.

We humans are magical creatures. So far, we are the most intelligent race of beings that we have found in the universe. We are capable of love, sympathy, empathy and joy. We should be celebrating ourselves, and each other, every day.

Instead, we seem to spend our whole lives fighting something or the other. These conflicts have gone on for generations, and they will continue for generations to come.

We were all born equal and we were born to live a happy life. Why can't we live in peace and harmony, happily ever after?

BEING HUMAN

'OUR APPROACH HAS BEEN TO TRY AND CREATE MERCHANDISE THAT YOU CAN USE IN EVERYDAY LIFE AND THEREBY DO GOOD IN THE COURSE OF LIVING YOUR DAILY LIFE. FOR EXAMPLE, WHEN YOU BUY A BEING HUMAN T-SHIRT OR A BEING HUMAN WATCH, YOU DO GOOD JUST BY THE ACT OF SLIPPING ON THE T-SHIRT OR STRAPPING ON THE WATCH.'

–SALMAN KHAN

When Salman Khan launched this initiative, 'Being Human', it confused me a bit. At the time, he didn't really explain the thought process behind the initiative. He may have mentioned that proceeds would go 'to help the cause of the underprivileged', but not much more than that. He just launched a colourful line of T-shirts with 'Being Human' printed in scrawling type across the chest.

But within a very short span of time, millions of people had 'Being Human' scribbled across their chests. Coming from the marketing and consumer industry, I was shocked to see people from every strata of society sporting the phrase. In a single day, I would see a kid at a traffic light wearing the T-shirt and begging for change, a chairman of a large MNC wearing the T-shirt for his early morning walk on Marine Drive, and an Israeli with dreadlocks wearing the T-shirt, sleeves cut off, on a domestic flight to Goa.

Was it the star power of Salman that caused the T-shirts to sell to so many different people? Personally, I don't think so. His star power hasn't really proved bankable for brands or sponsors. He's not usually at the top of a company's endorser wish list, far behind the likes of Shah Rukh Khan and M. S. Dhoni.

Was it the cause itself? Did people want to buy these T-shirts because they knew that it was making a difference? I really doubt it. Firstly, because it's really, really f?@king hard to motivate people to spend their money for the reason that it will help someone.

Secondly, because, like I said in the beginning, there was very little communication of what the Being Human Foundation was going to do with the proceeds. Even now, on the website, there is no clear plan of how the money that the foundation is earning is being spent. 'Proceeds from the activities of these initiatives go towards spreading education and healthcare for the underprivileged' is about all the explanation there is.

I think that the success of the merchandise line is due to the power of the words themselves—'Being Human'. The meaning of those words, the impact of those words, is what gets the attention of so many different classes and creeds of people.

I think that Salman touches upon a very basic fact that we take for granted. Despite all our differences of skin colour, religion, class, we are all formed from the same basic DNA. We are more similar than we are different. We are all human. But by stating it so simply, so factually, so in-our-f?@king faces, he makes us ask an important question: what does it mean to 'be human'?

In our day-to-day life, in the rush to get to work on time, to meet our deadlines and to save up enough money to trade in the C-class for an E-class, we don't ever ask ourselves what it means to be human.

For me, being human means having the highest order of

intelligence, with an ever-evolving awareness of the physical and emotional connection that we share with all living things. And with this comes a higher level of responsibility for those other living things—animals, plants, the whole planet really, and of course, other human beings.

'Being Human' is a plea for us to start remembering who the f?@k we really are, and realize the power that we have to make a difference.

These are my thoughts on what it means. Not Salman's. Salman has never said what those two words mean to him. That's why I call his initiative a 'merchandise line' and not a campaign. A campaign is a concerted effort towards a social, political or commercial goal. He's got the commercial part down, for sure.

But if Salman, just by printing these two words on a T-shirt, has had such a commercial impact, imagine if he shared his thoughts behind the initiative. His commercial campaign could turn into a social campaign. He could follow his own advice, be human, and be the change. The multiplied effect could be massive.

Surely, Salman Khan does not have the time to read *F?@k Knows*, but if he does end up doing so someday, I sincerely request him to turn his merchandise line into a campaign.

Brother, take some time out, gather your thoughts on what being human really means to you, and to the world, and share it. You've certainly got our attention; now tell us what you mean. What are you hoping to achieve? Call us to action. Don't just sell us the words—make us believe in them.

The author, for the record, appreciates and celebrates the thought of Being Human, by Salman Khan.

THE GURU IS WITHIN YOU

'ACT. DON'T REACT.'

You don't need a mentor. You don't need a guru. You don't need a priest. Everything that you need to know, the answers to any question that you will ever ask, is within you. Your guru is within you.

The only reason that you don't already know this is because it is not in society's best interest that you believe in yourself. It's not good for the people in power because they can only thrive if you perceive yourself as somehow weak. It's not good for your government, which thrives on your fear of economic instability, the infringement of your personal rights and your fear of terrorism. It certainly isn't good for the church or the temple, who position themselves as your direct line to the Big Guy. It's not an ideal situation for the ten richest families in the world who basically control all of the world's wealth (you should definitely research this a bit more, it's quite fascinating).

Here in India, we have the Aastha Channel. It's the most popular religious television channel in the country. Hundreds of self-proclaimed spiritual gurus preaching and teaching all day, every day. They do a fantastic job of highlighting the weaknesses of the human mind, prophesying the consequences of these weaknesses, and then offering a solution. But the solution always has a price. It is either to buy the guru's special herb-and-spice vitamin blend, or to be indoctrinated into the guru's special formula for happiness.

That's what the gurus are promising—happiness and success. What they are selling are techniques, meditations, medicines, potions, pamphlets and books. You can buy as much as you wish, you can subscribe completely to their brand, but at the end of the day, even they admit that the happiness is already there inside you. Just as they find guidance within themselves, you can find guidance within yourself too. All they can help you do is find it within yourself.

For you to subscribe and grant them the power to help you, they first need to prove to you that you don't know how to find your inner guru yourself. It's another catch-22. 'Your guru is there within you, but you aren't strong enough or smart enough to find it yourself (even though a guru should be pretty much all-powerful).' They kill your chances of discovering your guru for yourself, and then attempt to show you their way.

Our education system is the same. It kills your self-confidence from the start. 'You are dumb, we need to teach you. You don't have to decide how to behave, we will tell you exactly how to behave. You don't have to ask any questions of your own, we will give you the questions, and the answers!'

In my humble opinion, and you don't have to buy anything from me (any more than this book, which you have, presumably, already bought), the only thing that you have to do to discover the guru within you is to break free from all the social conditioning that you have undergone. Everything that your teachers, preachers, politicians and gurus have instilled in you, you have to forget. Throw away the self-doubt, throw away the fear, and go back to listening to your heart.

Your guru is within you. Don't let anyone else tell you otherwise.

ONE SEAT ON THE AISLE, PLEASE

'THE DEFINITION OF A GOOD TIME,
IS WHEN YOU DECIDE TO HAVE ONE.'

The frowny-virus has spread into the malls and movie theatres. Recently, I bumped into a bunch of super-intelligent, upwardly mobile people talking intensely amongst themselves outside a theater. No one was smiling.

They had just finished watching *The Rum Diary*, which stars Johnny Depp. I happened to know one of the guys in the group, and as I walked up to say hello, I heard them cursing the f?@k out of the movie, the director and Johnny Depp. I mean some really hard-core abusing.

I said, 'Whoa! Dude, why the hell are you so pissed off?'

He said, 'Man, you have no idea! That was *the* shittiest movie that we have ever seen.'

I said, 'Did you watch the entire movie?'

He said, 'Yes.'

'Did you have some popcorn and soda?'

'Yeah, yeah we did.'

'Did you pay for the ticket?'

'Yeah...'

'Did you step out from your house to come see it?'

'Yeah...?'

So I said, 'Dude, Johnny is not an asshole. You are a f?@king asshole. After making a conscious decision to watch a film, travel across town, spend $25, use four precious hours of your life for a cinema experience, you choose to whine about it!'

He had not just one, but two bottles of Tabasco, green and red, up his ass.

I stopped going to movies with other people. I realized that, if I walked into a movie theatre with any expectations at all, I would, for sure, walk out disappointed. If I went without any hopes or expectations, then I was sure to have a good time. I enjoy the cinema experience and if the film happens to be outstanding, then it's a total bonus.

I have an illness, in that I observe everything. Nothing escapes my attention. So if someone else accompanies me to the movie, I see their energy, I absorb their expectations. No thanks. I would rather be alone. And if I go alone, I buy the ticket for the seat next to me, too. I shouldn't have to listen to some stranger mumbling—'Oh, are you kidding? That wouldn't happen. No way!' during the movie. It affects me.

They say the path to spiritual enlightenment is found by breaking the identification with the mind. By detaching. By becoming the observer, instead of the actor. Being the audience in the movie theatre of the mind, watching your thoughts, desires and fears play out in 70mm. Not reacting, not identifying with the characters, but just simply…watching.

That's how I watch movies! Dirty B-grade, Hindi movies, contemporary Shakespearean drama, cheesy romantic comedies… I don't judge. I just enjoy the cinema experience. Other people's expectations and reactions to a film affect me, but the film itself? I can watch absolutely anything, and enjoy it.

If I can watch a movie that way—unbiased, unreactive, without any expectations—then just imagine if I can do this within my mind as well. If I can transfer my ability to watch a movie without judgement, if I can focus that inwards and do the same thing with my mind's eye, then, f?????@@@@@k, I would have really arrived! I could be the next Buddha!

But, sitting under a tree for the next forty years sounds pretty frickin' boring. Maybe I can be the next Osho! Inspiring people to renounce all religions and follow their own journey to enlightenment. But then to die of mysterious causes? Hmmm... maybe not. The next Jesus? I can't believe I even said that.

Forget it. I'll just enjoy the newfound enlightenment by myself. Peacefully, quietly. Happy just knowing that I am so much more f?@king sorted than everybody else.

The end.

THESE ARE A FEW OF MY FAVOURITE THINGS

'I LOVE TUNNELS THAT HAVE A HOLE AT THE END.'

I know you younger lot out there are trying to establish yourself in the world and seek to prove your individuality by including either really bizarre, really violent, or really freaky movies on your 'OMG! I looove that movie' list. Movies like *The Tree of Life* (what the f?@k was that?), *Saw VI* (are you serious?), or *The Human Centipede II* (I swear to God, if you like that movie you are one sick f?@k).

I, however, love the tug at your heartstrings, restore your faith in humanity, always a happy ending, learn a life lesson, cinema classics.

These are a few of my favorite movies, and what they have taught me:

1. *Notting Hill*: Love makes life beautiful.
2. *Jerry McGuire*: Find your space. And 'Show me the MONEY!'
3. *Cinderella Man*: Focus can move mountains.
4. *Invictus*: Self-belief is all you need. And the power of sport for social change is immense.
5. *Three Idiots*: You only have one life.
6. *Rocky*, parts I, II, III, IV and V: Impossible is nothing. And

there is no pain without gain. And, 'If I can change, you can change, everybody can change.' And, 'Nobody owes nobody nothin'. You owe yourself.'

7. *Iron Man*: There is a superhero in each of us.
8. *The Matrix Reloaded*: 'Some things change, and some things don't.'
9. *Braveheart*: You can lead, if you don't want to follow.
10. *Life Is Beautiful*: Life is beautiful.

YOUR BODY IS YOUR TEMPLE

'YOUR BODY IS YOUR ONLY UNCONDITIONAL
PARTNER IN LIFE, COME WHAT MAY.'

You've surely heard the saying, 'Your body is your temple.' It's a simple, but powerful thought. You can't worship inside, if the temple is falling to pieces around you. Your heart and your mind can't be strong and healthy unless your body is strong and healthy.

F?@k knows why looking after your temple is not your most important occupation. For a majority of people, physical caretaking is at the bottom of the priority list. It's a big reason why the grumpy virus runs so rampant through the population today. Weak bodies leave the heart and mind susceptible to all sorts of afflictions.

Is your temple well-constructed and fortified against weather changes and potential disasters? Are the pipes clear and flowing? Is the wiring laid correctly? Are the lights on, ready for you to turn inside at any moment, and take a brief respite from the wicked world outside?

It's not that hard to find out. In the morning, after you look into the mirror and introduce yourself to yourself (I'm totally sure that you are still doing that, right?), just take off all your clothes and check yourself out.

Give yourself a two-minute, buck-naked fashion show in front of a full-length mirror with all your brightest, whitest light bulbs on. Prance back and forth. Do a slow pirouette, and take a good long look from top to bottom. Are you happy with what you see?

What aren't you happy with? Most women will usually find more faults than necessary, and I'm definitely not the right person to give advice to them (and I would be too scared to even mention the word cellulite). Most men on the other hand—well, mostly straight men—aren't usually as critical of themselves as they should be. They let themselves get away with too much. I do have a few tips for the guys out there.

Shailendra Singh's
Signs that You Should Hit the Gym

1. Your boobs are bigger and bouncier than your girlfriend's.
2. When you reach up to grab the single malt off the shelf, your hairy beer belly plays peekaboo with anyone around to see.
3. You call in sick to work for one whole week because the elevator in your building is broken.
4. She's always on top.
5. If it's anything less than a five-hundred-rupee note, you leave it on the floor where you dropped it.
6. You need a Red Bull just to walk to the chemist to get your cholesterol medicine.
7. You wear only flip-flops, so that you don't have to tie your shoelaces.
8. You weren't able to look at yourself naked in the mirror when I told you to.
9. You cannot see your own penis when you urinate.

So, what do you say, guys? Feel like a good cardio session right now?

Keeping track of your internals is not as hard as it seems, either. No one knows your body better than you do, but we've all just stopped paying attention. If you have heartburn after a meal, you've eaten too much. If you never know what time you are going to have to run to the loo, then you need more fibre in your diet. If your lips are dry and cracking, drink some more frickin' water, and moisturize.

It's not rocket science. But it's too easy to just pop a pill for that headache, drop a few poisonous Otrivin drops into your stuffy nose to eat away the mucus and your brain cells, or snort a few whiffs of that Vicks VapoRub inhaler. In the long run, all that stuff will do more harm than good. But we all do it, because we're too lazy to make the necessary adjustments.

It's simply about making time for the important things in life. And there are very few things that are as important as keeping your body strong and fit. What good is all that money, all those cars, all those houses, if your body falls apart before you are able to retire and enjoy them?

And, tell me, how many cultural icons, how many great achievers, how many rock stars and superstars can you think of who are beer-bellied, blubbery and sloppy? Maybe some French royalty (a lot of people called 'King Louis'), a few American presidents, Winston Churchill, Elvis (later), Oprah. But, for the most part, I don't think it's a coincidence that the majority of personal heroes are healthy and fit... Bruce Lee, Bob Marley, LeBron James, David Beckham, Jason Statham, Dr Dre (have you seen him lately?).

Only when your body is healthy, and you aren't always fighting aches and pains and fatigue, can you start to focus on the health of your mind and of your soul.

You know it's true. You know you have to take better care of your body and spend more time ensuring your health. Don't wait until something bad happens.

Take care of your body. Take care of your temple.

It will also help you to pick up hotter chicks.

RUNNING ON A TREADMILL

'WHERE THE F?@K ARE YOU GOING?'

I met a friend at the gym. He was running like mad on the treadmill. I mean, seriously going mental—forty-four minutes into a run at a speed setting of twelve. Drops of sweat were flying, empty water bottles were tossed on to the floor.

I couldn't help myself. 'Yo, dude! What's going on? How much have you run?' I asked as I slapped him on his wet shoulder.

Proudly, he said, 'Almost ten kilometres.'

'Wow,' I said. 'Where have you reached?'

'What?'

'Where are you going?'

'What?'

'Where are you going?'

He got really angry. He punched the big red STOP button, grabbed his towel and turned to me. 'You asshole. I get your f?@king point. I ran eight kilometres, but I am exactly where I started. Now, f?@k off.'

That was funny. But even more hilarious was that, when he left the gym, he got stuck in traffic. It took him thirty-five minutes to travel the three kilometres to his house.

♦

We live in the city to be close to the business, the money, the entertainment, but it takes us hours sitting in traffic just to get down the street. We stack our homes one on top of the other, growing vertically towards the sky, but are we getting any closer to a higher purpose? We are eliminating parks and playgrounds to build malls and multiplexes, trading life-sustaining organisms for entertainment. We install sunrise- and sunset-replicating artificial lights in the house, since the smog of our daily energy consumption blocks the real thing.

I think you've realized through this book that I am a fairly optimistic person. I think that, by focusing more on the 'good', you can combat any of the 'bad'. But commuting through the Mumbai havoc every day to work, or wherever you currently reside, and considering the quality of life we are currently living, I do feel a pang of concern.

Are all these sacrifices really worth it? F?@k knows.

I've been running hard, and I've been running fast. I've built companies. I've built brands. I've thrown huge parties and charity events. I've entertained. I've competed. I've given back. I've run the miles, but how far have I really gotten?

I haven't yet had the guts to push the big red STOP button. But, I have been slowly, slowly reducing my speed. Bringing down the incline one step at a time. I'm not sure exactly what's going to happen when I jump off the treadmill, but, at this point, I kind of feel like I'll be happy just to get somewhere. Anywhere. It doesn't really matter, as long as I'm not still right where I started when I finally stop running.

RICH/WEALTHY

'IT'S NOT ABOUT THE MONEY YOU EARN,
BUT HOW YOU HAVE SPENT YOUR MONEY,
THAT MATTERS.'

Are you rich? Or are you wealthy? Which do you ultimately aim to be?

Don't know the difference? Let's check with the authorities: Merriam-Webster Dictionary defines them (I've included only those definitions that are applicable to our discussion), as:

rich *adj*
1: having abundant possessions and especially material wealth
2a: having high value or quality b: well supplied or endowed
<a city *rich* in traditions>

wealthy *adj*
1: having wealth: very affluent
2: characterized by abundance

With 'wealth' being defined as:

wealth *noun*
1: abundance of valuable material possessions or resources
2a: all property that has a money value or an exchangeable value
b: all material objects that have economic utility

Understood the difference? Yeah, me neither. So, let's check the

Merriam Webster Learner's Dictionary. These definitions are for those learning English, describing the word within the most commonly used context:

rich *adj*: having a lot of money and possessions

wealthy *adj*: having a lot of money and possessions

Hmmmmm…that didn't really help, did it?

Shall I tell you what I think the difference is?

'Rich' means that you have a lot of cash, but that you are not really culturally or traditionally mature enough to handle it. Rich people use their money to buy all the latest and most expensive toys, up-and-coming real estate to flip for more money, and to go to all the restaurant and club openings in the city and buy buckets full of the most expensive champagne. The rich are super-consumers.

If you are 'wealthy', then not only do you have money, but you are culturally and traditionally arrived enough to turn that money into wealth by investing in property, art, antiques and heritage items. You don't just buy things with the highest price tag because it looks good. You buy things that have a history, that mean something to you, things that have a soul.

In a way, I believe that it is the money that you have earned, that makes you 'rich'. It is the money that you spend that makes you 'wealthy'. Wealthy is the state of mind that you get from using your riches for your enjoyment.

Also, what's the point of having all that money, if you don't spend it while you are alive? You can't take it with you. When you die, you won't be remembered for the amount that you earned. No one, except for your wife, will go over your accounts and tally up how much money you made in your life.

But they will remember you for what you spent that money on. Did you spoil your children? Did you build an incredible art collection? Did you fund some amazing charitable projects? Did you use that money to fulfil all the dreams that you had for this life? Accomplish all the goals that you had set for yourself?

You won't be remembered for your riches. You will be remembered for the wealth that you created in your own life, enjoyed, and then left for the next generation.

My father had saved all his life. He made us travel in buses, and we only went out to dinner on very rare occasions. It was only when he was on his deathbed, in the hospital, that he wanted to pass on all the money he had saved up all his life, for a rainy day. He wanted to write checques to all the people he loved. But, by that time, he could barely grip the pen. He struggled to write the first few cheques to his sons, and couldn't finish the rest of them.

He didn't have time to give it to all those whom he loved. He didn't take it with him when he left. So, the government took it for taxes.

Are you rich, or are you wealthy?

FIT/HEALTHY

'FIT IS A STATE OF MIND.
HEALTHY IS A STATE OF HEART.'

What's the difference between being 'fit' and being 'healthy'? Merriam-Webster Dictionary defines them (I've included only those definitions that are applicable to our discussion), as:

fit *adj*
3: sound physically and mentally

healthy *adj*
1: enjoying health and vigour of body, mind, or spirit
2: evincing health <a *healthy* complexion>

With 'health' being defined as:

1a: the condition of being sound in body, mind, or spirit; *especially*: freedom from physical disease or pain **b:** the general condition of the body <in poor *health*> <enjoys good *health*>
2a: flourishing condition

Understood the difference? Yeah, me neither. So, let's check the Merriam Webster Learner's Dictionary. These definitions are for those learning English, describing the word within the most commonly used context:

fit *adj*: physically healthy and strong

healthy *adj*

1a: having good health: not sick or injured
 b: showing good health

Right…that didn't really help, did it?
Shall I tell you what I think the difference is?

On an early weekday morning, I was training at a very popular Mumbai gym. A youngish—maybe around thirty years of age—but fattish gentleman walked into the gym and straight up to the reception. With a very sincere expression on his face, he requested the attention of the manager of the gym.

'Excuse me. Manager? I'm getting married in fourteen days, please fix me a routine that gets me to look like this, in time for my wedding.' I'm not even going to tell you what the man in the photograph looked like! He continued, 'This is very important. Please take this seriously.'

'Fit' is a quick fix. It's a specific physical goal that you have in your mind, in the short term, that you work towards achieving. You plan and use specific techniques to be able to look a certain way (six-pack abs) or be able to do something (run a marathon). 'Fit' is about the packaging. And the way that we live our lives nowadays, that's pretty much all that matters.

One of my clients-turned-friends, an actor (no names, sorry, or he would seriously have me shot), flew to Cuba and got himself an eight-pack, biceps and shoulder cuts. It took fourteen days and who knows how many surgeries. He came back looking like a midget Arnold Schwarzenegger. F?@k knows what's going to happen to his insides after all that drastic surgery.

These guys wanted to get 'fit' in a hurry. They didn't give a shit about being healthy.

'Healthy' is a constant state of being fit. It's about doing what is best for your body, all the time. Or at least, trying your best not to do any harm to your body, most of the time. It's not about how you look in the mirror; it's about how you feel inside. It's about listening to your body, understanding what it needs and what it likes. If you really listen, your body will tell you exactly what it wants to consume. That communication is actually the primordial origin of the 'gut feeling' that we keep talking about. The body's very basic dialogue: 'Is this good for me, or not?'

These people the masses lust over—the poster boys, the muscle heads—they care more about looks than they do about holistic health. They feel that looks matter more than internal fitness. They want a six-pack, not a good regulatory system. They may look good on the movie posters with their shirts off, but you do realize that they can't actually use those bodies, right? They can't bowl a cricket ball, because their arms don't rotate all the way around. They can't dance (with the exception of Hrithik), because their bodies only stiffly click from position to position. They can't even wear regular clothes, because their bodies are so misshapen after all that contortion. I even know one famous Bollywood star who only poses for the camera facing one side, because one muscle-packed arm is freakishly bigger than the other one. He also has noodle legs.

They can only stand there and look pretty.

Thanks, but I would rather get out on the cricket field, run through the grass and throw some hard, fast bowls. I would rather have the stamina and the flexibility to attempt all the poses of the Kama Sutra. I'm happy to be able to cross my arms across my chest to indicate anger, or boredom. I'd rather my insides worked properly, than have some freakishly enhanced 'V' muscle pointing to my crotch.

I'd rather be healthy.

HAPPY HEARTBEAT

'PAIN, ANGUISH, FEAR, STRESS AND ANXIETY ARE ALL JUST
STATES OF MIND.
YOUR SOUL IS ONLY HAPPY.'

Our body, heart and mind define our existence. They each have an important job, but it is only when these elements are in balance that we can truly live a beautiful and happy life.

Your body is the temple of your heart and mind. We've talked about the importance of treating your body well. If you put good things in, you will get good things back. If you constantly maintain it, it will remain strong and healthy for a lifetime. We've talked about how, if your heart and mind are not fully happy, then the effects will show on your body.

Your body needs to be strong and uncontaminated to keep your mind clear and your heart at peace. In today's age of door-to-door transportation, nine-hour workdays sitting in an Aeron chair, minute rice, and lack of wild predators, it does take a bit of effort to keep it fit and fortified. Your body also works hard to keep itself healthy: filtering pollution, fighting off infection, balancing on five-inch heels, digesting Big Macs, french fries and Cokes.

We've talked about the mind in previous chapters. Its job is to observe, consume and store its findings as data for use in future processing. If you leave your mind wide open and free, it will absorb every piece of information, every bit of knowledge and experience, with no judgement of whether it is good or bad for you, and file it all away. Without any conscious control over inputs, your mind can use all of that data to make you feel confused, insecure and afraid.

If you consciously restrict what information you accept, using Chi F?@k Po, you can filter the data and store only what you want to keep. If you maintain conscious control over the mind, then it will use the good information to help guide you and create a greater sense of awareness. We've discussed how you need to tell it to 'shut the f?@k up', or switch it to airplane mode and give it a rest, otherwise your heart will never have a chance to speak.

Your heart, on the other hand, has a less complicated function. It simply has to keep beating. One beat after the next. Just keep on ticking. As long as your heart is beating, you are still alive. But the heart does something more, something that we too often ignore, which is just as important to maintain.

The heart lets you know exactly what the body and mind are up to.

Your body and mind can be mischievous f?@ckers. The mind wants full control of everything, and wants credit for being the supreme ruler. The body just wants another body to bang up against, most of the time. Their actions are not as pure as the heart.

The heart can see right through to the intentions of the body and mind, and it loves to snitch. You don't need a polygraph test to read it. If you listen closely, if you keep a clear channel of communication open with your heart, it will tell you, with each beat, the inner calculations of your mind and body.

If your body is lying in a hammock, swinging gently, and your mind is only wondering what to do with all the ripe mangoes you can hear falling in the forest, then your heart beats slowly and steadily. Your heart is as relaxed as the body. If a cobra comes sliding under your hammock, your body tenses in apprehension, your mind starts plotting fight-or-flight options, and your heart starts beating rapidly, ready to pump adrenaline through your veins at the moment you need it most.

When you are in love, and your body is fully attuned with the body of your lover, and your mind runs parallel to theirs, then your heart beats as if it is beating for them, in sync and purposeful. When you lose someone you love, your heart starts to beat irregularly, like it really doesn't give a shit and is happy to stop beating, if you want it to.

If you can hear your heart, if you can wake up in the morning and, with your eyes still closed, feel in your chest a happy heartbeat or a sad heartbeat or a scared heartbeat...then you know the entire state of your being.

◆

When I shattered my thumb in seven places, I was sent into an operating theatre for the very first time. The theatre was cold, the lights were bright and doctors and nurses were running briskly everywhere. Apparently, if they didn't open up and reset my thumb soon, it would shrivel up and fall off.

The surgeon was a good friend of mine. 'Shail, Shail, Shail...' he tsked. 'Took your eye off the ball? Not like you.'

I laughed, 'Ha ha. No, doc, it was a googly. I got googled.' Although, in truth, he was right. In an incredibly rare moment of distraction, for the first time since I started playing cricket—I'm not lying, I am super focused on the field, it's my meditation—I had taken my eye off the ball. I never take my eye off the ball.

He laughed, I cracked more jokes. He promised me just one shot of anaesthetic in the neck, and I had to rip him a new asshole after he gave me eight more. After the ninth shot, however, a nurse quickly came to his side and whispered something in his ear. His eyes looked up from the needle to meet mine, pointedly. 'Are you okay, Shailendra?'

'Sure, doc, all fine. What's going on?'

'Yes, yes. You do seem fine to me. But your blood pressure is up to 198 by 142.'

'Uh-huh. And what does that mean?'

'It means that you are a few seconds off from a brain haemorrhage or cardiac arrest.'

'Holy f?@k!'

'Indeed. Please open your mouth. I'm going to give you a few drops and you will...'

Before he finished, I was unconscious, floating through dreamland.

Just goes to show you. You can look fine on the outside, strong and smiling, but your heart does not lie. It registers the intense fear that you are fighting, the fear of hospitals, the fear of pain. It feels the agony that your body is going through, trying to keep the bits of your thumb together. It feels everything and does its best to warn you, notify you, help you. You just have to keep listening.

When you are a child, your heart is clean and honest. It beats with exhilaration at the new world you are discovering, and with surrender to each moment. Except when hungry, hurt or wanting a new toy ('how does it feel to waaaaaant?'), a child is happy. Their heart beats happily.

But as you grow up, as you start to collect the expectations of your family, your friends and society, your mind starts to turn manic, struggling to keep up with the pressures and contradictions and compromises. Instead of following the heart, the mind starts to lay its burdens on the heart.

You stop going outside to play, stop (literally) chasing girls, stop using your hands to build skyscrapers out of blocks and then using your legs to kick it to the ground—and your body becomes less nimble. Television serials and reality shows replace hide-and- seek and sliding down the stairs in onesies. Alcohol, cigarettes, coffee and carbonara sauce make you pack on the pounds. Stress and saturated fats clog your arteries.

Your heart really starts to feel the pressure.

During the time that I was slowly losing my father, fighting the epic legal battle in the Middle East, and coping with the lingering effects of the economic crash of 2008, I had a standard medical check-up.

My doctor said, 'You seem fine. All your tests are normal. But I have to tell you, your heartbeat doesn't sound exactly right. I can't tell you specifically what it is I notice, there's no scientific term that's applicable right now. I can't prove it, but, if you trust me as your doctor, then just take my word for this.

'Your heartbeat sounds...stressed. It's not your usual, comfortable heartbeat. It's like, when you first sit in your car, turn on the engine, and let the car warm up. As you listen to it idle, when you feel its vibrations, you know everything that you need to know about your car. You might not even consciously hear anything wrong, but you know when it's "not right". You can feel when something is amiss.

'Shailendra, something is amiss in your heart. I think we should run some further tests.'

They gave me every heart-related test they possibly could and they all came back back clear. Two months later, I was admitted to the ICU with 95 per cent blockage and a near fatal heart attack.

Your heart contains all the happiness in the entire universe.

You just need to make sure that your heart remains in control, and doesn't become a pawn to the mind and body. If your heart remains the centre of your universe, you will know exactly who you are, and what you want. Your life will be fulfilled and you will be content.

It's all in your control. Seriously. No matter what the world throws at you, no matter how much stress and anguish and pain it throws your way, if you practice your Chi F?@k and take in only what you want, if you keep your mind steady, calm and under control, and if you fortify your body against the hazards of misuse, then your heart will beat strong and steady. It will beat happily.

The choice is yours. Don't you want a happy heartbeat?

HAPPILY SAD

'BEING HAPPY AND BEING SAD ARE BOTH EMOTIONS THAT WE CREATE AND EXPERIENCE. WHY THINK OF ONE AS GOOD AND THE OTHER AS BAD?'

Have you ever celebrated being sad?

Sadness is an incredibly intense emotion. It's a powerful connection with your inner self.

Tears come from a deeper place. Deeper than laughter. Laughter is an outburst of noise that overwhelms your mind and makes it pause. Laughter brings silence to the mind by default.

Tears bring a more profound silence. A deliberate silence. A silence of realization.

It's an extraordinary moment when you feel something so intense emerging from deep within your soul. You will learn something about yourself when you cry. You will know yourself better. And *that* is always worth celebrating.

ANOTHER TIP

Worrying is like riding a tiger. If you can stay on top of it, you will enjoy the ride. If you get off, the tiger will eat you.

HOPE IS POISON. DON'T WE F?@KING KNOW THAT?

'MY UNCLE WANTS TO BE AN AUNTY. MY DOG WANTS
TO BE A CAT. MY CAT WANTS TO BE A LEOPARD.
THE RICH WANT TO BE POOR. THE POOR WANT TO BE
POLITICIANS. THE GUILTY WANT TO BE INNOCENT.
AND THE INNOCENT ARE STILL LIVING ON HOPE.'

We spend so much of our precious time *hoping* for things, when actually, the possibilities lie in our own hands. We can make anything happen. Impossible is nothing. But, for the most part, human beings are lazy f?@kers. If given the option, we'll usually take the easy way out. And so we end up 'hoping' for things.

Instead of saying 'Just done it!', we say: 'I hope I pass the exams.' 'I hope I get the promotion.' 'I hope I don't get her pregnant.'

If you f?@king study hard and know your subject, you will get good grades. If you have identified and applied your best skills and made an effort in your career, you will get promoted. If you wear a condom, not only will you not get her pregnant, but you will also not get her chlamydia.

'Hope' is a very dangerous word. If you always hope for everything to just fall into your lap, it actually makes you a very hopeless person. You basically don't have the balls to go out there and make it happen for yourself. You look to someone or something outside of you to bring you luck. You start believing in strange rituals, reciting prayers to catch the attention and blessings of an unseen God floating in the clouds. You start ringing bells and lighting incense, disturbing a long list of other gods and begging them to fulfil your dreams for you.

For the gods' sake and for your sake, drop 'hope' from your vocabulary and take charge of your own destiny.

'To "expect" in this life
is to beg with a bowl called "hope".'

CHEER THE F?@K UP!

'WHEN YOU GET F?@KED, YOU GET ANGRY.
ARE YOU NOT TRYING TO GET F?@KED ALL YOUR LIFE?'

Why do you spend so much of your time being miserable? I mean, shit, dude. You do! Face it, you are miserable most of the time. Or, if you aren't miserable, you're at least *not* happy.

You have so much to celebrate. You are alive and breathing. You have fully functional senses, limbs and organs. Or, if you don't, if you are differently abled, then you seem to have managed pretty well so far. You have sufficient food and shelter. If you have disposable income to buy this book, then you probably have some trendy, branded clothes and the latest limited edition sneakers on. You have adequate spare time to sit down and read a good—well, halfway decent—book.

Then why the f?@k aren't you smiling? Why do you seem so bloody hassled all the time? Like this existence is such a terrible burden. Like it's a challenge to even wake up in the morning and step outside into the sunshine.

Why aren't you happy? Why aren't more people happy?

Here's my theory: totally unscientifically unproven, but believed fully, from the tangled depths of my gut... *They* don't want us to be happy. Society needs us to be unhappy. If we are happy, we don't want more. And if we don't want more, then we aren't being good consumers.

Being good consumers means that we spend lots of money on things that we don't need, earn more money to fund that spending, and empower the government to govern us so that we can protect the money that we earn and spend. We also empower the government to protect our financial interests and to give us access to things that we do absolutely need, especially if they are located in other countries. Things like, oh, maybe... oil, located in the Middle East?

Consumerism is not just about what you buy and own. I am not recommending that you sell your Ferrari and your house and live out of a tent on the beach. I, personally, believe that you can have your cake and eat it too. If you want a Ferrari, and work hard to earn enough money to get it, and it makes you happy to buy it, then by all means, buy the Ferrari!

Consumerism is more about what you *don't* have and the feeling of insecurity that arises because you don't have it. That is what society thrives on. It wants you to believe that your life is complicated, stressful and an endless competition to be bigger and better and stronger and richer. If you are never satisfied, if there is always something more that you want and aspire for, then you will continue to earn money, spend money, and require higher powers to protect the whole system.

It's not about 'wanting more', it's about *how* the wanting more makes you feel. It's a good thing to want more, if it makes you work hard to save up money and buy something that makes you truly happy. It's a good thing if wanting more makes you create new ideas that transform industries and help you soar to great heights in your career, if it makes you happy. If buying a Porsche fulfils a childhood dream and puts a big-ass friggin' smile on your face, then it's bloody f?@cking good for you!

But if wanting more makes you feel frustrated, anxious and

fearful, then it's bad. If the feeling of not having something makes you insecure, that's bad. If buying the hottest car or the coolest phone makes you happy only until you realize that a cooler model has come out and then you hate yourself for not waiting one more week, that's bad.

Life is about enjoying what you have and wanting to have more to enjoy. Consumerism is not enjoying what you already have and longing for what you don't have. It's as simple as that.

Now, take a good look around you. What do you have? Do you have people who love you? Do you have a roof over your head? Do you have clothes on your back? Do you have food to eat? Clean water to drink? Are you breathing? What do you lack?

Cheer the f?@k up, man! Life is good.

A SMILE A DAY KEEPS THE GRUMPY VIRUS AWAY

'A SMILE TAKES YOU MANY MILES.'

My profession allows me the privilege to travel the length and breadth of the globe. I've been everywhere from The Louvre in Paris, to Johnny Depp's office in Los Angeles, to the Masai Mara in Tanzania. I know the layouts of all the major airports, and I can tell you the airlines that hire the hottest airhostesses and serve the best biscuits.

In the last ten years, though, I've been noticing something about my fellow travellers. I don't know if I am getting more observant, or if I care more, or if it's really true, but...everyone looks f?@king miserable.

Whether it's in the London tube, or the duty-free shop in Hong Kong, or on a flight from Delhi to Chandigarh, people look as if a bottle-full of Tabasco sauce has been stuffed up their ass and they are just waiting to get home to wash it out. Foreheads are creased, noses are turned up, the corners of lips turned down. People look like life has ridden 'em hard and put 'em away wet.

London folks look especially miserable with their raincoats buttoned all the way up and their noses buried in a book or a newspaper. Everyone is always reading something or the other, so I can understand why they are generally thought to be intellectuals. Their handle on basic math tells a different story, however.

New York City subway riders haven't seen a tree or more than a half-hour of sunlight a day for years. Their daily cup of coffee and bagel with cream cheese costs five times as much as the $1.25 a day considered to be the marker of the poverty limit. They can't cross the street before the almighty green hand tells them it's okay. That's probably why they're so miserable.

Mumbai commuters either have their face jammed into someone's armpit on the train, or are sitting in their air-conditioned, chauffeur-driven car, stuck at the Worli Naka signal, calling all their friends and talking about how miserable it is to be stuck in traffic. Most of them have to piss also, but they know they don't have a chance in hell of finding a public bathroom anywhere from 'town' to Bandra.

It's just as bad on flights. The world is getting smaller. You can go anywhere, be everywhere. But everyone is f?@king miserable while getting there! And, everyone's in a bloody rush.

Just seventy years ago, it would take three months of travelling on a barge with rotting food, un-bathed, stinking travel companions and decks full of rats to get from India to England. Now you just have to sit patiently and quietly for seven hours on a Boeing 747 before you reach your five-star in London. Chill the f?@k out, man!

Would it hurt you to smile at the person sitting next to you? Is it really so painful to say, 'Hi! How you doin'? Where ya goin'?' Are you afraid they might waste a few minutes of your valuable time telling you about themselves? They might have a cool story to tell. You're packed like a sardine on a tiny plane seat. You can't turn on your iPod or iPad until the plane takes off. Do you have anything better to do than hear a good story?

It's a virus of unhappiness. I call it 'the grumpy virus'. You can see the symptoms everywhere. Where's the celebration of life? Where's the satisfaction of living in the moment, whenever the moment may find you?

And, let me not generalize. I am speaking to those people most likely to buy this book and read it. Upwardly mobile, decently to well-educated, working middle class. A huge part of India's population. It's you f?@kers that never celebrate. (Celebrating is not going to a nightclub every Friday, spending a good chunk of your salary on overpriced cocktails and going home with a person you just met.) You don't attend Laxmi pujas at your workplace any more (the place where your money comes from), you send birthday greetings over Facebook or via text message, and when was the last time that you sent your mentor a small gift on teacher's day?

You know who does celebrate? The other 50 per cent of our population; while living in the slums, surviving hand-to-mouth, lacking opportunities and access to the most basic living requirements. But they know how to party! Any birthday, marriage, anniversary, achievement, and especially holidays! If Ganesh and Laxmi and Shiva and Ram are watching over us, well then, the meek are surely going to inherit the earth! If the gods are just a myth and this is our one and only shot, then that 50 per cent is completely enjoying the ride.

Me? I smile at everybody and I make conversation with almost everyone I meet (unless you are coming to ask me for free Sunburn tickets). From a taxi driver in Oxford, to the popcorn seller in a theatre, to the receptionist in a hotel. It's a blast hearing people's stories.

Just last week, a Mumbai taxi driver told me that the reason he loved working in the city is because you never know who you might see. One day, many years ago, he saw his favourite actress crossing the street in Bandra.

'I actually saw her! Sridevi! Can you imagine? I was so excited, that I told my wife back in UP. Four days later, my wife showed up here in Mumbai, and has never left. I came here, sharing a room and a taxi to make more money to send home, but now I have bought an independent flat and my wife has had three children.' Was it worth it, to see Sridevi? He sighed, 'F?@k knows.'

Apart from the entertainment and insight I get from hearing other people's stories, I always step out of the taxi feeling more… human. I feel connected to all the people whom I cross paths with in a day. And that makes me feel like a part of something larger than my own life.

Long story short: smile, my friend! Greet your fellow human beings with a pleasant grin and a 'Hello!' Dump grumpiness! You have so much to be glad about. All the people on this planet are potential friends, if you just give them a chance. Smile and the world will smile back at you. ☺

SWEETLY CRACKED

'IF YOU'RE HAPPY AND YOU KNOW IT AND YOU REALLY WANT TO
SHOW IT... DON'T.
THE WORLD MIGHT HATE YOU FOR IT.'

You know how *they* say 'smile, and the world smiles back at you' or 'a smile takes you many miles'? Well, I just wanted to warn you that they might be exaggerating a little bit.

I know that reading this book has been bringing you joy. I know that you are finding it surprisingly enlightening, while being thoroughly entertained. I know that this book is making you, overall, a much happier person.

So, I must give you a word of caution, before you go sharing your newfound happiness with the rest of the world. See, the thing is—it's very sad, but—people don't like to see other people really, really happy. You would think your friends and family and co-workers, at least, would feel glad to see you genuinely joyful. But, no, they usually don't.

When you are super happy, people start thinking that something must be wrong with you. Because it's so against the norm, something must be awry. People don't like people who have a blissful look on their face and a delighted smile playing on their lips.

Again, you don't need to be a rocket scientist to figure out why. They're jealous. They're deep in the trenches of consumerism, wanting what they don't have. If you are so happy, it must mean that you have it all. That makes them more insecure and anxious. If you appear blissful and content, then they are angry because you must have been given, or have found, or bought something that they don't yet have to make them happy too.

People love people who are stressed out, frowning, chain-smoking cigarettes and smashing them out in an ashtray. Those people are 'edgy'. They're 'real'. They don't have enough, still hopelessly want more, and other people can relate to that. It makes them feel better that they haven't found it yet either.

'Life's a bitch and then you die. Right, dude?' Puff. Puff.

You'll be excited to share your joy. But people will push back. They'll cock their heads and ask you, 'Why are you always smiling? Why can't you take photos like a normal person?'

I, however, wish you an incredibly happy and beautiful day. I haven't asked much from you so far, just a few minutes looking in the mirror in the mornings and quiet time to make your F?@k It List. So, do me this one little favour.

Today, have the f?@king balls to have a really great, happy day. I want you to be happy. If you can't find reason to celebrate on your own, then do so in honour of me. Because today, I am goddamn ecstatic! I wrote a book, and you are reading it! That makes me friggin' ridiculously happy.

For a guy who hates to read, forget about writing, I made a superhuman effort to write this book. Why? Because it made me f?@king happy to write it. Simple. I followed my heart, appreciated the experiences that I have been through, and I wrote them down in a book that someone is actually reading.

Today, there is nothing more that I could ask for. Today, I feel fully alive. I only want the same for you. Nothing would make me happier than knowing that, after you have read these substantial chapters, you cheered the f?@k up, grew yourself some cajones and headed out into the world to make yourself happy.

Don't give a shit if people think you are a little bit mad. It's best to be a bit mad. Sweetly cracked. Leave the rest of them to their sorrow and despair. You and me, we'll go f?@king party! Gangnam style.

HAPPY BIRTHDAY TO ME

'LIVE LIKE A SHOOTING STAR, PARTY LIKE A ROCK STAR,
DIE LIKE A SUPERSTAR!'

Your birthday. Now that's a f?@king day to celebrate! For so many reasons.

1. You survived another year!
You avoided the 'Eenie meenie miney mo' of destiny. You escaped the arbitrary crushing of your head under a bus or having a fish bone stuck in your throat. You didn't throw yourself off a bridge in depression or get stabbed in the face by a jilted lover.

F?@k knows what all could have happened to you in the year past! But you made it! Woo-hoo!

That's worthy of celebrating your birthday with a huge-ass party. Midnight to early morning with a lot of friends and ridiculous amounts of expensive alcohol.

2. You are one year closer to death! Woo-hoo! Yippee!
No, really. As I have said, numerous times before, only when you accept the fact that you are going to die, will you really start to live. Your birthday means that you are one year closer to death. And hopefully, it means you will get even more serious about living the life that *you* want to live. 'Cause you are running out of time, baby.

I would also recommend celebrating the afternoon after

the big party. By yourself. Go to your favourite temple, church, synagogue, mosque, tarot card reader, whorehouse—wherever you find the most peace—and take a while to reflect upon your situation.

Did you accomplish the things on your yearly F?@k It List? Did you avoid all the things on your F?@k Me, I Don't Wanna Be List? Do you know who you are? And what you want? Are you happy?

If you don't celebrate reason number two peacefully, on your own, and you only do the binge drinking, debauchery part, then it kind of seems like you are throwing a party for being one year closer to dying. It seems a little funny that everyone is coming to eat your food and drink your liquor and feel happy that you are now going to die sooner than you were going to last year.

3. This is more of a rethink than a reason. I, personally, think that your birthday party should be thrown in honour of your mother. She's the one that carried you in her womb for nine months, pushed your big-ass head out of her hoo-ha and then raised you up from a screaming little brat to a big, whining idiot.

Don't forget your mom on your birthday. She's the one who did all the work.

F?@K KNOWS IF DEATH IS NOT AS BEAUTIFUL AS LIFE

'I HATE THE WORD "SIN". WHO'S JUDGING ME?
UNDER WHAT CRITERIA?
AND WHY AM I PRESUMED GUILTY UNTIL PROVEN INNOCENT?'

I have always wondered how, since none of us have seen death, it has been so vividly presented to us throughout history? Death can only be experienced after you are f?@king dead, no? So, who has been reporting back?

Somehow, someone seems to be getting information. Death has been pretty well documented. Universally, there are two extreme views on what we're in store for, after death.

The pleasant vision of the afterlife is that it is an endless bright whiteness, with a sense of weightlessness and quiet. Angels and halos and lack of want for anything. There are reports of being connected to everyone and everything at the same time. It's been said that, when you reach the gates of heaven, all the pets and animals that you have ever loved will come running out to greet you.

At the other end of the spectrum, there are much darker images of the afterlife. One in which everything is consumed in fire and brimstone. Souls are lost in a deep, dark forest, full of grotesque people tearing off each other's limbs to fight over food and water that never really quenches hunger or thirst.

From a human aspect, I can understand how these images have been constructed and used to the benefit of religions all over the world. To keep people living in fear and, at the same time, give them hope, so that they look to them for guidance in the right direction. These images have appeared in countless religions, in some form or another, across countless civilizations since the beginning of time. Where are these ideas coming from?

F?@k knows. I don't believe that I have any way to know the answer to this. So, I'm not going to stress myself thinking about it. I'll eventually find out, right?

Basically, in my view, there are only two possibilities.

The first possibility is that my soul will go on living in another dimension or in other forms. Most gurus say that this is damn good fun, and actually give up their bodies to speed up that process. To continue on my journey with my soul freed from the burden of the body, is a mind-blowing prospect. Who hasn't, at one time or another, felt that their body is a prison, restricting the spirit?

The second possibility is that the atheists are right: when your body dies, your life is extinguished. No body, no soul. No heaven, no hell. Game over. That doesn't really seem like such a bad option. No pain, no conflict. Just…nothing. What's to worry about in that?

I really don't think I will be eternally damned to hell, or forgiven for all my sins and sent through pearly white gates. That seems too…analogous to this human life. Too convenient. It must be more mind-blowing than that!

If you really asked me to give you my gut feeling on the matter, I would tell you that I happen to believe in the gods. I have interesting conversations throughout the day and night with the different gods that I believe in. It makes me feel nice. If the gods are there, well then, there must be life after death.

Otherwise, where are they all chilling out while they wait for me to send my respects?

I don't know if I've been influenced by all the references to the afterlife through the ages, but I visualize it as a place of pure happiness, huge parties, lots of champagne, no politics, no economics and no earth below your feet. You're flying all the time. Always happy. I don't want to sound stupid and morbid, but I'm quite excited to experience the other side. I think it's going to be awesome.

Like I said, I'll find out eventually.

In the meantime, what's most important is that when the end does come, I want to be able to say that my life was beautiful. With all its anxieties, happiness, anguish and magic, I just want to be able to say that, 'just to breathe was joy itself'. To say, 'I have lived. I have loved. I have done everything humanly possible in this lifetime. I have expressed myself. I have created. Now I am ready to taste death.' Sooner or later, whichever comes first.

I can't think of a worse hell than looking back at my life, while still alive, and realizing that I didn't make the most of it.

F?@K KNOWS
WHY I WROTE THIS BOOK

I can't believe that you actually read this book all the way through! So, what did you think?

I'll go first... In my opinion, ladies and gentlemen, what you have just read is the most inconsistent, contradictory, non-articulate piece of writing that I have ever read.

That being said, this book has come straight from my heart. I followed my gut, I stopped thinking about doing it, and did it. Even if it flops, I have so thoroughly enjoyed the journey of writing it. I did it with a happy heartbeat. I gave it my 100 per cent.

Himmat-e-marda madad-e-Khuda.

I was nervous and petrified to put this out there. I'm not an intellectual. (As if you couldn't tell from my references to popular movies and the fact that I mentioned corn poop.) I have terrible writing manners. I had nightmares of real Indian authors—Deepak Chopra, Amitav Ghosh, Salman Rushdie—sneaking into my room in the middle of the night to suffocate me with a pillow for what I might do to the reputation of writers from India.

But, f?@k that! I did it. 'Just done it!' I wrote it! And you read it! I made a passion my latest profession, and now I'm a bona fide author! I gave, and you have received. You have been healed through the therapeutic powers of Chi F?@k and Chi F?@k Po. You have found the guru within you. You have shut the f?@k up and are following your heart. You have a F?@k It

List! Welcome to the club of ordinary 'F?@k Knows People'.

I hope you are all laughing with me right now. You better not be waiting to f?@king cry for me when I die. I've got no time for that. Life is short. I'm going to celebrate until my very last breath.

I'd like to sign-off this book with the following, very profound thought.

You will read, but not understand.
You will understand, but not do.
You will do, but not understand what you did.
Does it make a difference?
F?@k knows.

F?@k knows if this will be continued...

ACKNOWLEDGEMENTS

I would like to celebrate a few very extraordinary people, who have had a strong influence on my life and the journey of this book.

My father, the legendary, loving, best friend, and mentor, Late Mr Mangal Singh.

My mother, Mrs Saroj Singh.

My brother, Harindra Singh.

My Rock of Gibraltar, my wife, Nayana Singh.

My best friend and one and only son, Shaan Singh.

My right hand, my left hand, and my middle hand. Aditya Motwane, Abhishek Nayar and Danny Mamik.

My first draft readers, Raveena and Reshu.

I couldn't be more fortunate than to have David Davidar as my editor and Kool Kapish Mehra as my publisher.

And last but not the least, my partner in crime, my co-writer and the co-soul of this book, Nicole Sottung. (No chance that I could have done this without you.)

Love you all! Thank you!
Jai Mata Di!